If I Ever Get Back to Georgia,
   I'm Gonna Nail My Feet to the Ground
Don't Forget to Call Your Mama . . . I
   Wish I Could Call Mine
Does a Wild Bear Chip in the Woods?
Chili Dawgs Always Bark at Night
Don't Bend Over in the Garden,
   Granny, You Know Them Taters Got Eyes
When My Love Returns from the Ladies Room,
   Will I Be Too Old to Care?
My Daddy Was a Pistol, and I'm a Son of a Gun
Shoot Low, Boys, They're Ridin' Shetland Ponies
Elvis Is Dead and I Don't Feel So Good Myself
If Love Were Oil, I'd Be About a Quart Low
They Tore Out My Heart and Stomped
   That Sucker Flat
Don't Sit Under the Grits Tree with Anyone
   Else but Me
Won't You Come Home, Billy Bob Bailey?
Kathy Sue Loudermilk, I Love You

Comedy Albums

On The Road with Lewis Grizzard
Lewis Grizzard Live
Let's Have a Party with Lewis Grizzard
Addicted to Love

You Can't Put No Boogie-Woogie on the King of Rock and Roll

GRIZZARD

You Can't Put No Boogie-Woogie on the King of Rock and Roll

VILLARD BOOKS · NEW YORK · 1991

All rights reserved under International and Pan-American Copyright Conventions. Published in the United States by Villard Books, a division of Random House, Inc., New York, and simultaneously in Canada by Random House of Canada Limited, Toronto.

Villard Books is a registered trademark of Random House, Inc.

The contents of this work originally appeared in *The Atlanta Journal and Constitution*.

LIBRARY OF CONGRESS CATALOGING-IN-PUBLICATION DATA
Gizzard, Lewis
You can't put no boogie-woogie on the king of rock and roll/
Lewis Grizzard.—1st ed.
p. cm.
ISBN 0-679-40601-8
I. Title.
PN6162.G787 1991
814'.54—dc20 91-15315

Manufactured in the United States of America
9 8 7 6 5 4 3 2
First Edition

To my goddaughters, Joanne and Gabby.
And to the unborn child of my friend
Mike Matthews, who swears if it's a boy,
he'll convince his wife to name him
Michael Lewis.

Contents

15 ONE-SIZE-FITS-ALL GOVERNMENT

16 STUCK IN THE SAND IN THE MIDDLE EAST

Introduction

The Geesinslaw Brothers are a country-music and comedy act out of Austin, Texas. I've been a fan since I first discovered them. During my college days at the University of Georgia.

They had a song with the line "You wouldn't put no shuck on me, would you?"

The phrase, in its purest definition, means, "You wouldn't lie to me, would you?"

But it also can be expanded, as in:

- "You wouldn't shit me, would you?" A good response to somebody saying, "Do you know professional wrestling is all fake?"
- "You sure you're not making all this up?" What you might say if a male friend was giving you a detailed account of having sex with the entire University of Oklahoma cheerleading squad. Just the girls. If he had taken on the entire squad, you might say, "Good God, Harvey, I'm never going to shower with you at the club again."
- And, "Sheee-yet," which is Southern for "I ain't believin' a word of that."

And then it goes into another sphere, the one that indicates you know the whole thing's nothing but a lie, and you're too smart to believe a word of it.

These phrases come to mind:

- "I didn't just roll into town on no turnip truck."
- "When do you think I was born?"
- "Spot's died" (from Dick and Jane).
- And, "You can't bullshit a bullshitter."

All these phrases are protective devices against any and all forms of attempted verbal chicanery.

I only recently came upon what I consider to be the best of any of the aforementioned, however. I was on the first tee at the Ansley Golf Club in Atlanta with my foursome. We were discussing the bet and handicaps. One member of the foursome said he was a 14, and we knew damn well he was nowhere over a 10.

I said, "I didn't just roll into town on no turnip truck."

My partner, Bob (Puddin) Johnston added, "Hey, you can't put no boogie-woogie on the king of rock and roll."

I loved it. Somebody told me later there was once a song with a title like that. I could never substantiate that, and I don't care if that's where Bob Johnston got the line. It's still a great line, and I remain impressed he came up with it at such an appropriate time.

I told Bob as we drove down the first fairway, " 'You can't put no boogie-woogie on the king of rock and roll.' I'm going to use that as a title for a book one day."

And so, here we are.

Usually, when I turn out a compilation of my newspaper columns for a book, I get all my columns previously unpublished in a book, and throw them into the air.

Then, I reach down and pick them up randomly. When the stack feels heavy enough to be a book, I send them to my editor in New York City, and he sends me an advance check. And you thought books are complicated.

But I liked the title of this book so much, I actually took great pains in the selection of the material you will be getting to soon, if you will bear with me for only a few more lines.

I am not a modern man. I am a fifties and sixties child. I basically haven't understood anything that happened in or to the world since 1963, the year I turned seventeen.

Kennedy got shot that year, and then the Beatles appeared, and before I knew it, they were passing out condoms in schools, putting mushrooms on cheeseburgers, and singing songs with a lot of bad words and no melody. Rap, which brings up another phrase one can use as a means of implying disbelief and a certain amount of disgust: "Rap, my ass."

So the following pieces have at least traces of that sort of string that ties them all together. Well, maybe not all of them. But most. I wouldn't try to put no shuck on you.

I enjoy writing about things that baffle me. Why do young men wear their caps backward nowadays? What's the government doing running a whorehouse? Why is *Nightline* showing a Madonna video? Why doesn't anybody name a child "Norbert" or "Ernestine" anymore? Why can't I call Iraqi troops "towel-heads" and "camel jockeys"?

Or, "What the hell is all this, and I'm too smart to let them get away with it."

Read this book and I am satisfied it will be hard to get anything by you again. You will learn not to take anything without first dissecting it completely.

You will suspect no one, you will suspect everyone. You will assume nothing blindly.

Reading this book probably will also help you financially. Sure, it will cost you a few bucks, but you probably won't ever buy a used car again. You won't believe it's necessarily true just because you read it in *The New York Times* or saw it on the local news. And you definitely will lose some trust in your stockbroker, which could save you untold financial miseries.

That's about it, except for one last story about not getting any boogie-woogie cast upon thy person.

You can use whomever you want when you retell this story. I first heard it told with racial overtones, but I would dare not use such here. I'm a Georgia Dawg, so I can use two of our most hated rivals, Florida and Auburn.

A Florida guy reads an ad in the paper that says, "Vacation Cruise: $99."

He goes to where they are selling the tickets and says to the guy, "I'm here for the ninety-nine-dollar vacation cruise."

The guy says, "Okay, that'll be ninety-nine dollars."

The Florida man forks it over. Then, the guy comes from behind the counter and knocks him unconscious with a baseball bat. After that, he bundles him up in some blankets, ties some rope around him, and throws him out the back into the river.

An Auburn guy comes in a few minutes later, pays ninety-nine dollars, and gets the same treatment. The bat, the blankets, the rope, and he's thrown in the river, too.

Fifteen minutes later, the Auburn man and the Florida man are floating down the river together.

The Florida man says, "I wonder if they're going to serve any food on the cruise."

The Auburn man replies, "They didn't last year."

1 MODERN LIFE

Frankly, I lost a lot of respect for the Lone Ranger when I found out what "kemo sabe" really means—"sweetie pie."

Reality Bites the Bullet

Remember how cowboys in western movies could get into a fifteen-minute gunfight and never have to reload their pistols?

In case you're too young to remember western movies, that happened all the time.

Growing up, I must have seen twenty Roy Rogers movies, and I never recall Roy ever running out of ammunition.

Of course, the Indians rarely ran out of arrows either, and the other thing I always wondered about was when an Indian spoke English, he never used articles and never referred to himself as "I."

Tonto would never have said to the Lone Ranger, "I think I'll go over and water the horses."

He would say, "Me go water horses."

I realize a certain economy of the language is often necessary, especially when one is involved in the high-minded business of making certain that good triumphs over evil.

But it seems to me, the Lone Ranger would have finally gotten tired of the way Tonto spoke and said to him, "Listen, Tonto, this 'Me go water horses' thing has got to stop.

"In the future, please use the pronoun 'I' when you refer to yourself, and throw in a 'the' occasionally."

I bring up the past to make a comment about movies of today.

A lot has changed in the area of movie weaponry. Very rarely do movies today involve the old western six-shooter. Mostly they involve assault weapons, weapons that will spit out a bullet a millisecond, weapons that crazies buy when they want to wipe out some kids on a playground.

But in the last couple of modern shoot-'em-ups I've seen, namely *Die Hard*, with Bruce Willis, and *Lethal Weapon II*, with Danny Glover and Mel Gibson, I've noticed another flaw reminiscent of the you-never-need-to-reload-a-six-shooter.

In *Die Hard*, Bruce Willis, a lone cop against a group of terrorists in a high-rise office building, must have had at least a thousand bullets fired at him, some at very close range.

But was he ever hit by a single shot? No.

In *Lethal Weapon II*, more people got shot than live in medium-sized towns in Kansas.

I admit Mel Gibson finally got hit at the end, but not enough to kill him—so we can look forward to a *Lethal Weapon III*, in which every living thing in Salt Lake City is blown to bits.

If terrorists and drug dealers and South African bad guys spent two hours shooting at you with automatic weapons, you're probably going to wind up dead in a real world.

Do you know what I think? I think the National Rifle Association is behind all this somehow and is trying to give the subtle message that it's no use to ban assault weapons because the good guys aren't going to get hit anyway.

It's time Hollywood realized its responsibilities and had a few stars shot up to prove bullets don't discriminate between good guys and bad.

In the immortal words of Tonto, "Me go water horses. You stay here and get head blown off."

Yo ... Can You Cap This?

Add this to the long list of things I don't understand about modern culture:

Why are so many of today's young men wearing their ball caps backward?

Surely others have noticed this, too. I don't have any scientific figures, but I would be willing to guess that at least 75 percent of young men who wear ball caps are wearing them backward.

I used to wear ball caps. But I always wore them the way I figured God and whoever invented ball caps intended—with the bill in front so as to keep the sun out of my eyes and off my face.

The only person who wore his ball cap backward was the catcher. He had to turn his cap around in order to wear his face mask.

But when he wasn't behind the plate, he turned his cap around like everybody else.

Wearing ball caps backward seems to have no racial lines. I've seen both young black and white men wearing their ball caps backward.

I stopped a young black man and asked why he was wearing his ball cap in such a manner.

He said, "Yo."

So I stopped a young white man and asked him the same question.

He said, "Yo," too.

I'm not certain what "yo" means.

Perhaps it means, "I am making a statement that says I refuse to adhere to ancient customs of adults, and if I want to wear my ball cap backward, I will continue to do so, yo."

Later I saw a young man wearing his ball cap with the bill in front.

I said, "Does this mean you are not making a statement and refusing to adhere to ancient customs of adults?"

He said, "Yo, I knew something didn't feel right," and turned his ball cap around backward.

I still have an old ball cap. I keep it around for sentimental reasons. I was wearing that cap when my high school baseball coach came to the mound one day when I was pitching and said, "Grizzard, you couldn't get your grandmother out. Get off the mound."

I put my old ball cap on my head and then turned it around with the bill in the back. I looked like a skinny Yogi Berra, or Joe Garagiola when he still had his hair.

I turned it back around. I looked like a forty-three-year-old man who couldn't have gotten his grandmother out.

I've come to a couple of conclusions in this matter.

One is that I probably shouldn't question the customs of the younger generation in the first place. My generation, when it was still young, made its own statements. We wore ducktails and rolled up our Lucky Strikes in our short sleeves. We were trying to say, "My, but is that Jerry Lee Lewis a piano-playing fool?"

And, two, young men who wear their ball caps backward probably should carry a card around in their wallets that say, "If I have been injured and rendered unconscious, please don't try to turn my head around."

Yo, you never know.

Inventive List of Gadgets

One of the best things about living in these times is that hardly a day passes there isn't word of some new gadget that will make our lives a little more interesting. Look at what's happened with the telephone. First came call-waiting and call-transferring and 900 numbers you can call to hear your horoscope, get ball scores, or get talked dirty to.

Now, there is a service available that tells you the phone number of the person who is calling you. This is great. All I have to do is compile a list of the numbers of people I don't want to talk to, and when they call, I can ignore the phone and go back to my shower massage.

Can you imagine what new gadgets are on the horizon? Leonardo da Vinci predicted airplanes long before there was even the Greyhound bus.

This fact gave me the incentive to sit down and make out a List of Things That Might Get Invented by the Year 2000.

My list:

- Electric boxer shorts: You take off your boxer shorts, toss them on the floor, and they walk to the washing machine, wash themselves, then walk back and fold themselves neatly in your boxer shorts drawer. Great for any guy who no longer lives with his mother.
- Booger alarm: If you happen to have a visible booger in your nose, say just before you go to pick up your date, the alarm goes off, saving you a great deal of embarrassment.

- Cordless lie detector: You carry it like your booger alarm. It will be small enough to conceal in your vest pocket or in your purse. When somebody is lying to you, the alarm goes off. This will be especially helpful when buying a used car or talking to your stockbroker.
- Wapnerizer: You plug it into your television and when *People's Court* comes on, it tells you how Judge Wapner will rule on each case before the commercial break when he goes back into his chambers to decide which creep he's going to stick it to.
- Quayle-o-meter: It keeps up with all the dumb things Vice President Quayle has said lately so you won't miss a single one.
- Robot marital-argument settler: You and your spouse get into an argument you can't settle. You turn on the robot, it listens to both sides and then determines who is right and who is wrong. Made with an indestructible material so it can stand up to getting hit with a heavy object by the loser.
- *Wheel of Fortune* decoder: Not only does it solve the puzzle before any letters are guessed, it also tells you what color panties Vanna White is wearing and how much longer Pat Sajak's talk show can possibly stay on the air.
- Electric Roach Motel: The minute a roach decides to take a bath in its room, the maid unlocks the door, plugs in a hair dryer, and then throws it in the tub, instantly frying the roach.
- Number-calling scrambler: Attach it to your telephone and when you call somebody who doesn't want to talk to you (because he has the gadget that gives him the number of the caller), it messes up the system and indicates the call is coming from his mother.

When he answers, "Hello, Ma?", you can say, "Gotcha!"
The nineties should be a real hoot.

"Klutz" Is My Middle Name

A great many Americans are severely impaired when it comes to operating modern-day gadgets.

I've read that 68 million American households have VCRs, but 80 percent have no idea how to operate them.

I'm afraid I fall into this category. I have two VCRs. One sits on the top of my bedroom television. I have another on top of my living-room television.

A friend came over and hooked them up. Afterward, he showed me how to set the timer and insert the tapes and all that.

For a fleeting moment I thought I had it. I set the timer to tape a movie the following afternoon so I could watch it in the evening.

But I must have put the tape in backward. All I got was a lot of black, squiggly lines on a field of fuzzy gray. Stewart Granger was in there somewhere, but I couldn't find him.

I was afraid to use either of my VCRs after that. Others go to video stores, rent movies, and then bring them home and enjoy them on their VCRs.

I use mine for something to set houseplants on.

I believe God is responsible for the fact I am mechanically impaired.

The day before I was born, he was telling the angel in charge what sort of personal traits to give me.

"Okay," God began, "Grizzard. Let's see. Give him skinny legs, poor eyesight, but allow him to still have his hair into his forties.

"One other thing. Don't give him the ability to operate anything more complicated than a comb."

Unfortunately, a lot of people aren't smart enough to operate the gadgets that are supposed to make our lives easier.

Here are some other things I can't do.

- Remember to put the plastic top back on my coffeepot, so the coffee will float into it from the automatic coffee maker.

  What happens in that case is that coffee stays in the filter holder and then runs out and makes a mess. I would use instant coffee, but I don't know how to turn on my stove to boil water.
- Operate my electric toothbrush. I put toothpaste on it and turn it on, and it begins to vibrate violently and slings all the toothpaste onto my bathroom mirror.
- Successfully remove a cork from a wine bottle by using a corkscrew. I now buy my wine in cans. Are you supposed to sniff the pop tops?
- Open a childproof container of aspirin.
- Set a digital alarm clock.
- Remember how to hold dental floss correctly.
- Operate any sort of typing mechanism you have to plug in.
- Turn on a Jacuzzi.
- Remove the top of a can of dog food with my electric can opener. Luckily, black Labs can eat right through a can.
- Operate the fax in my office at home, the one I got for Christmas when what I really wanted was some new 33-rpm Big Band records for my Victrola.
- Dance the lambada.

But I still have my hair, and I probably will be able to keep it as long as I never try to dry it in my microwave again.

Why Johnny Can't Read Nothin'

I was watching one of those Sunday news programs on television, and the subject was, in essence, what dummies some American students are.

A high school senior was asked when the Vietnam War ended. He didn't have the foggiest.

A high school girl was asked if she knew what the Holocaust was.

"A Jewish holiday?" she asked back.

Statistics also were introduced that, among other things, said a large portion of today's high-schoolers don't know Mexico is our immediate neighbor to the south.

Then, a panel of experts discussed what was wrong with our educational system, and what could be done to improve it.

There is no doubt some weaknesses exist in American education, but you can't put all the blame on teachers and administrators.

Some must go to the students as well. If you are seventeen and don't know who's south of the border, it means you are, in fact, a dummy, and no matter what quality of teaching you are getting, you'd still be a dummy.

I sat down and thought about why so many of today's students are dummies. Several reasons come to mind. I will list them:

1. Listening to Loud Music: What I think is this sort of thing damages kids' hearing, and when their teachers explain that

Mexico is our southern neighbor, they think she said, "The Holocaust is a Jewish holiday."

2. Orange Hair: Some kids dye their hair orange. Nobody who's stupid enough to dye his or her hair orange could retain any knowledge beyond where to go to get your ears pierced.

3. Computer Screens: Some of today's students spend a lot of time staring at computer screens. This fouls up their ability to see, as listening to loud music damages their hearing. When the teacher pulls down a map and explains where Mexico is located, they can't see the map, and they hear only a mumbling sound and think she's giving tomorrow's assignment, which is, "Everybody go out and dye your hair orange."

4. Music Videos: How are you going to interest students in history and geography when they can watch MTV and see a lot of sex? "When did the Vietnam War end? Who cares? Yesterday I saw Madonna mostly naked."

5. Sex: Studies show many students today start active sex lives at a very young age. They want to go home and study when the head cheerleader has gone into heat.

6. Drugs: You can't learn when you're on drugs, and you've got to be high on something not to get tired of rap.

7. In Conclusion: Are you a dummy? What is the president's last name, and where does he live? Where do you live? In what state is New York City located? Mary has an apple and eats it, how many apples does she have left?

How many schools are in the Big Ten? Spell "b-r-a-i-n-d-e-a-d."

Did you miss them all? Then you're a complete dummy, and good luck at Clemson.

Real Men Don't . . . Don't Do What?

The other day I read an article about a Conference on Men and Masculinity. I think it is a grand idea to hold such a thing.

Over the past couple of decades, a lot of men have had to ask themselves a lot of tough questions about masculinity, such as, "Should I keep wearing boxer shorts or switch to bikini briefs?", and, "Should I get some curtains for this place?"

Masculinity used to be a simple thing to define. If you had hair on your chest, a deep voice, and belonged to a club that excluded women, you were masculine, or, as was the phrase of the time, "a man's man."

But all that changed. The feminist movement came along, and suddenly women were saying they preferred Phil Donahue over Charles Bronson.

It was okay to be sensitive. It was okay to cry.

Dennis the Menace took down the sign on his tree house that read: NO GIRLS ALLOWED and welcomed Margaret inside.

Men's fashion rules changed. It was okay to wear pink. Then it was okay to wear an earring. Then it was okay for a man to wear his hair with a ponytail in the back.

But the new rules of masculinity, as I mentioned before, confused a lot of men, especially men my age, those who don't have enough hair left to make a ponytail in the first place and who are hurtling toward prostate trouble.

We learned masculinity from our fathers, our scoutmasters, and our high school coaches—veterans of World War II, stand-up guys who were against long hair and drank their beer from a bottle.

Our heroes were John Wayne and Aldo Ray. If Phil Donahue had been in our school, we would have beaten him up on the playground.

But look at us now. We are trying to fit in. Do we stay with Old Spice or switch to something with a name like "Dusk Musk"?

Do we use mousse (something we used to hunt) on our hair? Should we order a glass of white wine or stick with Budweiser? Should we discuss football when we are bonding, or the crisis in funding for the arts?

I overheard a comment made by a male friend the other day that is quite telling.

He's mid-forties, and he said, "I'm just glad my father didn't live long enough to see me playing golf with my wife on Saturdays and getting my hair cut in a beauty parlor."

As for my personal beliefs concerning masculinity, I have become more tolerant in the past years.

I have at least two male friends who have ponytails. One also wears an earring. They are still my good friends. I never ask them over to watch a tape of *Sands of Iwo Jima*, but they are still good friends.

I get my own hair cut where it's coed. I allow the waiter to pour my beer in a glass. I have a male friend who has a cat. I've stopped questioning his masculinity.

I believe women deserve equal pay with men. I read articles by women sportswriters. I don't believe there was ever a woman raped who was asking for it.

But I still wear boxer shorts, and the first time Margaret said, "You really should get some curtains for this place," it would be the last time she saw the inside of my tree house.

I haven't come that far, baby.

A Supercomputer
Meets Its Match

The human race is now in the debt of the Soviet chessmaster Gary Kasparov.

In case you might have missed the news, it was Gary Kasparov, the world chess champion, who went up against a chess-playing computer named "Deep Thought" and flogged the machine with relative ease.

It took the human two-and-one-half hours to win the first match. It took him only two hours to win the second.

And "Deep Thought," mind you, was no ordinary computer. It was, in fact, the World Computer Chess Champion.

What if the match had come out the other way? What if a computer had taken on a human in the complicated game of chess and had beaten him?

Wouldn't this have been a horrible blow to our self-esteem? If we couldn't beat a computer at chess, at what else might this thing with wires be superior?

Look at what computers have already proved they can do better than human beings.

They must be better at flying airplanes, because computers do most of the heavy work flying most new commercial jets.

Computers add, subtract, and divide faster and more accurately than do humans. Computers do most of the production work at newspapers today. Humans used to do that.

But Gary Kasparov's victory over "Deep Thought" proves we can still dominate computers in some areas, and that should offer some peace of mind to all of us.

I don't want to awake one morning and find out I'm working for a computer, instead of the other way around.

An editorial writer for the *Daily News* in New York obviously has this same thought and was appreciative of the Kasparov victory. The writer listed a number of things a computer still can't do.

My favorite was "purr." Cats can purr, and I've known women who could do something very similar, and who wants to pet a computer or hold one in his arms in front of a fireplace?

I was moved to make my own list of abilities computers don't have. The effort brought me much satisfaction.

A computer can't:

- Fry a chicken like my mother did, crispy brown on the outside, tender on the inside.
- Teach a small boy how to throw a curveball.
- Make a friend.
- Fix a flat tire.
- Deliver my newspaper to my front yard at the crack of dawn, 365 days a year without a single miss.
- Pat me on the back and say, "Great putt, partner," when I make an occasional birdie to win a $2 Nassau.
- Call a square dance.
- Get up and get me a beer when Southern Cal is threatening to score late in the game against Notre Dame.
- Sing "Angels Flying Too Close to the Ground" like Willie Nelson.
- Drive a truckload of goods from Spokane, Washington, to Nashville, Tennessee.
- Win a tobacco-spitting contest.
- Write a funny novel, like Dan Jenkins.
- Cry.
- Paint a masterpiece.
- Bake a cake.
- Have a baby.
- Save an earthquake victim.

Hooray for our side!

What's Ahead for the Economy

Some might scoff at the fact I consider myself quite the expert on the economy.

I am not without portfolio. I was treasurer of my freshman class in high school, and I take *The Wall Street Journal* at home.

I don't read it, but when friends drop by, they are impressed when they see my dog, Catfish, eating table scraps off the front page.

We've been hearing about certain economic indicators lately, and economists look at things like housing starts, retail sales, and the hemlines of women's dresses to predict what's forthcoming for the economy.

Over the years I have developed my own set of economic indicators, and they have proven to be trustworthy.

I was able to predict the stock-market crash of a few years ago.

A couple of days before the fall I tried to get in touch with my broker and got a recording saying his phone had been disconnected.

I knew that was a sure sign the bottom was about to fall out on the Amalgamated Goat and International Mushrooms he had sold me a couple of days earlier, and told all my friends, "Get out of the market."

They didn't listen, however, and a number of them now live in cardboard boxes.

What follows is a list of the indicators I use to tell me exactly what state the economy is in:

- Golf Tees: If you play golf, notice how many perfectly good tees have been left on tee boxes. If there are lots of them, then the economy is fine.

  People are in such good shape financially they don't even bother to bend over and pluck their tees out of the ground after they've hit.

  If there are no tees left, it means people are tightening their belts, and you might want to show up for work one day next week instead of lollygagging around on the golf course.
- Deion Sanders: If his monthly bill for jewelry drops under $100,000, tough times are ahead.
- Roach Motel: If you notice yours has a lot of vacancies each time you check in, even the roaches are feeling the crunch and staying home more.
- Tipping: If you leave your waiter a lousy tip and he not only complains, he also attempts to pistol-whip you, it's a sign you should be at home eating fish sticks instead of being out at a fancy restaurant.
- Ex-wives: If more than one calls in a single day to complain about the amount of alimony you're paying her, you can bet the price on such luxury items as pocketbooks and silky things they wear at night for their boyfriends has gone sky-high.
- Jesse Jackson: If a crisis breaks out somewhere and Jesse's not right in the middle of it making speeches, it means whoever picks up the tab to send him all over the world has decided to cut back.

My dog, Catfish, incidentally, thinks the economy is in sad shape. He's been eating off copies of old campaign literature lately.

My subscription to *The Wall Street Journal* ran out and I was afraid to reup. Jesse hasn't been in the Middle East in weeks now.

Pollution
Without Solution

The environment is supposed to be the main issue of the nineties, and Congress is already hard at work trying to figure out a way to do absolutely nothing about it.

I normally don't get involved in environmental issues, however, because they take too much thought.

It is much easier for me to sit around being concerned about celebrities falling off motorcycles, the spring-training lockout, and whether or not Andy Rooney is a racist.

(I think celebrities who fall off motorcycles deserve it, there are a lot of sportswriters up North who are going berserk because they are not in sunny Florida on expense account, and that Andy Rooney doesn't have a mean bone in his body until he is confronted by a paper clip he doesn't like.)

But if the environment is, indeed, going to be the primary issue of the nineties, I cannot sit idly by writing about mush while others are pondering the air we breathe, the water we drink, and whether or not the sun will say the hell with it one morning and not come up.

But if I am going to get into this thing, I want to get into it with both feet.

Sure, I know there's a hole in the ozone layer, tropical rain forests are disappearing, and trees pollute, but have you considered the following:

- Secondhand Alcohol Breath: If you are on an airplane for instance, and the person next to you is pouring down double scotches, you could get liver damage breathing this person's intoxicating exhales. The solution to this problem is to not allow Ted Kennedy on commercial flights.
- Polyester Pollution: Most people have gotten the word by now that polyester leisure suits are tacky, and they are taking theirs out into the backyard and burning them.

  The fumes go into the atmosphere and turn the rain purple, and that's why we are getting such freaks of nature like Prince.
- Fat Clouds: Everybody is losing weight these days. Where does this weight go? It goes up into the atmosphere, too, and forms big fat clouds, and if you were to be on top of a mountain and walk into one, you could come out with all that weight Oprah Winfrey lost, for instance, and suddenly have a rear end the size of a Buick.
- Depletion of the Pull of Gravity: It's happening. If it weren't, how could Don King's hair stand up straight like that?
- The Silent Sparrow Syndrome: If we don't do something to curb those car stereos that blare out music loud enough to be heard in three states, birds are going to quit chirping. What's the use? Who can hear them over The 2 Live Crew and their latest repugnant hit?
- The Bo-Knows-Where-It-Burns-and-Itches Problem: In the coming years we all will have watched 7 million Bo Jackson commercials on television, and the entire country could develop serious cases of jock itch through some rare form of electrical osmosis.
- The Bull-Hockey Factor: Scientists say that people who like to hear themselves talk, such as members of Congress, will have uttered approximately 17 septillion trillion pounds of bull-hockey by the year 1995, which can seep into your house through your air-conditioning ducts.

If we don't do something about that, nobody will be saying anything of substance by the turn of the century, and we will all sound like members of Congress talking about the progress of their latest environmental bills out of one side of their mouths while accepting lavish dinner invitations from oil-industry lobbyists out of the other.

2 GOINGS-ON

I don't know much about art, but I do know what a photograph of a man with a bullwhip in his rectum ain't. Art. This chapter deals with a lot of screwy things that have been happening in the world lately. It might be because of all those satellites we've sent into outer space. That's what caused the strange weather we had back in '69, according to my grandmother.

Hunkered Down
Against Terrorists

No reason to take any unnecessary chances during these tense times, so I've been preparing my house against a terrorist attack.

I really can't think of any reason a terrorist would attack my house, but you never know.

Perhaps terrorists sometimes just pick a place to terrorize at random or they blindfold one of their party and spin him around and around.

Then they tell him to walk, and whatever he walks into first, that's the spot they terrorize.

Sort of a pin-the-tail-on-the-infidel sort of thing.

The first thing I tried to do was buy a couple of gas masks for me and my dog, Catfish, the black Lab.

I went to K mart, but they were out of gas masks.

"Been a real run on them lately," the salesman said. "But could I interest you in a couple of Patriot missiles?"

Unfortunately, the missiles wouldn't fit in my car. I did buy a camouflage outfit and a can of green spray paint to put on Catfish in case we should need to hide behind the houseplants in my living room.

I wound up at Honest Gus's Used Gas Masks after that.

"I was in the used-car business before the war," said Gus. "Now," he went on, picking up a gas mask, "let me show you this little dreamboat. . . ."

I bought two masks, a clean one-owner for me and a '63 model for Catfish, most recently owned by a little old lady schoolteacher from Pasadena who used it only when she drove into L.A.

Then I picked up some canned food for storage. If terrorists used a chemical weapon in my neighborhood, I might not be able to leave my house for days.

I picked up a couple of cans of Spam for me and some Alpo for Catfish. I bought a couple of bottles of vodka in case the water became contaminated.

I also bought a handy book on frequently used Arabic phrases such as *"Be-bop, fallah, gunga, arahmafungo,"* which means, "Me? An infidel? Heck no, and neither is my dog, Catfish— which is English for Mohammad."

Of course, I'm also taking precautions against terrorists attacks while outside my house.

I have canceled all previously scheduled flights, for instance. Especially on Eastern. When fundamentalists, even Baptists, decide to force the pilot to fly us to Baghdad or the Shrine of Jimmy Swaggart in Baton Rouge.

Indications are that terrorists might target U.S. tourist spots as well, so I've also canceled an automobile trip to Dollywood in Tennessee, despite the fact there is a new museum there, featuring such artifacts as Dolly's first wig, and her training bra, which still has the original wheels.

I've also decided not to go near any military installations, oil refineries, or CNN headquarters in downtown Atlanta.

In fact, I think until this thing finally is over, I'll just stay in the house with my dog, Mohammad, and watch the mysterious Roto-Rooter van that's been parked across the street for a couple of days.

I don't mean to get hysterical or anything, but unless somebody tried to flush a gas mask down the toilet, nothing should take that long to unclog.

Say It Ain't So, Buffalo Bob

I've never cared much for the artsy crowd. They hold too many benefits, for one thing.

For another, they are the kind of people who would look at a photograph or a painting of a cat nailed to a telephone pole and say, "My, look at those lines," if it were hanging in a museum and somebody told them it was art.

The rest of us, of course, would say, "Good God. It's a cat nailed to a telephone pole. I think I'm going to be sick."

The artsy crowd currently is flitting about with great concern because of what it considers to be an effort by uncultured imbeciles to censor certain works it contends are not obscene, but of great artistic value.

There was Cincinnati where a museum showed photographs taken by somebody named Robert Maplethorpe.

The photographs were quite explicit. The artsy crowd looked at them and said, "My, look at those lines."

Others said, "Good God. I think I'm going to be sick."

A trial was held to decide whether or not a museum had the right to show the photographs.

The artsy crowd won, and if I had been on the jury, I would have cast my vote for allowing the museum to show anything it pleases, too.

Censorship in any form is wrong.

But that opinion doesn't stop me from saying that what's basically wrong with the artsy crowd is, it's full of it.

Sure, offer the photographs for those who want to gaze upon such. But don't try to pass it off as art.

One of the photographs in question was of a man with a bullwhip in his rectum.

During the Cincinnati trial the prosecutor asked the art director, who selected the photographs for the show, if he thought it depicted sexuality.

No, said the art director, it was a figure study.

Bullsomething else.

What it was was a photograph of a man with a bullwhip in his rectum, and no matter what the artsy crowd might call it, it's still a photograph of a man with a bullwhip in his rectum.

Doesn't common sense tell those people that?

Again, I'm not for censoring such a photograph. I'm just saying it's sleazy, filthy, obscene, decadent, and sick, and anybody who would call it otherwise is a damn fool.

At the recent Atlanta Arts Festival there was a puppet show, and at one point during the act, the puppets depicted oral sex.

Say it ain't so, Buffalo Bob. Puppets having oral sex and a photograph of a man with a bullwhip in his rectum.

If the artsy crowd doesn't awaken to the fact the rest of society isn't going to stop crying "smut" at such, then public support of the worthwhile might eventually stop, too.

The point here is, the artsy crowd can stick a bullwhip in its rectum and call it macaroni or anything else it wants to. Anything else but art.

At least we uncultured imbeciles recognize an old-fashioned maggot-gagger when we see one.

Accept Our Apologies, Mrs. President

What gets me about the women at Wellesley who said they were outraged by the choice of Barbara Bush as their commencement speaker is, Who do these little tarts think they are?

Barbara Bush is the first lady. Like Dolley Madison, a great American. Like Eleanor Roosevelt. Like Jackie, who was admired by the world.

Like Betty Ford, who proved to be one helluva tough lady. Like Rosalind Carter, the original Steel Magnolia. Even like Nancy Reagan, who ran the country during her husband's naps.

Okay, so it was with the help of an astrologer, but let's not get bogged down with details here.

Barbara Bush sleeps with the president of the United States, and it is extremely difficult not to be influenced by one's bed mate.

After the day's discussions, meetings, and briefings, it comes down to George and Barbara: When they're alone under the sheets, we must know the president occasionally asks of his wife, "What in the devil am I going to do about the situation in Lithuania?"

And even if he doesn't ask, don't you think Barbara, just after the lights go off, says to her husband, the president, "I've been thinking, George, and here's what you ought to do about, etc."

Barbara Bush, in other words, is probably the most influential woman in the country right now.

So where do a bunch of twentyish college students get the

high-handedness to say they are outraged because Mrs. President has been asked to speak to them?

So Barbara Bush has been a housewife and a mother and has gained recognition behind the achievements of her husband.

Didn't these women have mothers? How many of them stayed home to raise their children while the old man was out working his tail off to get the money to send them to a spiffy school?

Would they be outraged to hear their own mothers get up in front of their classmates and tell of the struggles they went through and the sacrifices they made to give their child a good home and an opportunity to educate herself rather than wind up a cocktail waitress?

To slap Barbara Bush in the face, as the Wellesley group most certainly did, was to slap a lot of other good and fine women and say to them, "You sold out by getting married and having kids and supporting your husband. You're not worthy of our respect."

I wonder where these children will be twenty years from now. A lot of them will be successful professionally, I'm sure. Perhaps there are future CEOs in the crowd. Maybe even the first woman president.

But how many of them will also leave their top-floor office suites and go home to a cat?

How many of them will be forty and rich and powerful, but won't have married, won't have had children, because they thought it was a cop-out?

So they are high and mighty now, considering themselves above hearing the wife of the president of the United States offer them a little advice, even if some of it might have been motherly.

That's a shame. Not everything was bad about the roles women of Mrs. Bush's era played.

There needed to be changes and there have been, but Barbara Bush has seen things and heard things and experienced things that could have benefited the women of Wellesley, and they have acted like juveniles.

I hope they all get big thighs.

Advertising for Sex

We have before us the case of a young woman from Fort Lauderdale who went out with her girlfriend one evening dressed in a sea-green tank top and a ruffled miniskirt. Actually, it's what she did not have on that is the key issue here. She didn't have on any underpants.

She gets raped by a twenty-six-year-old man, and then a jury ups and acquits him because, in the words of the jury foreman, the victim "advertised for sex."

Obviously, there have been outcries of injustice, and how can I remain silent when so many others have seen the wrong here and have made public their disdain for the obviously Neanderthal thinking of the jury?

Here's the deal:

You see a woman out in public dressed in a sea-green tank top and a ruffled miniskirt and you say to yourself, "Hey, this chick probably isn't wearing any underwear, either, which obviously means she obviously wants to do the dirty deed."

Okay, so there's some basis for logic there, I suppose, but here's the spoiler, Big Boy.

Just because she's advertising for sex, it doesn't necessarily mean she's advertising for sex with you.

She could be advertising for sex with her boyfriend, Harold, who's meeting her later.

She could be advertising for sex with her husband. Just because you're married doesn't mean you can't still be kinky. She even could be advertising for sex with a movie producer who might be hanging out and happen to see her, and a month from now, she'll be co-starring with Mel Gibson.

Here's all the jury had to know:

Did this woman want to have sex with the creep who raped her? The answer is, of course, no.

But, did the man force her to have sex with him?

The answer is, of course, yes.

Then it doesn't matter if she were walking around buck naked. To force someone into sex is rape, and it doesn't say anywhere that it doesn't count if the victim is provocatively dressed.

Send the creep to the Big House. If you don't, what happens the next time he sees a woman dressed in a sea-green tank top and a ruffled miniskirt?

If it were okay for him to rape the first one, why not number two?

Listen, I'm a man, and I know the stirrings that loosen themselves when I see a woman dressed in something she obviously isn't wearing to a Junior League meeting.

But there are ways a man can soothe himself when visited upon by such stirrings. Think of the least sexy thing you can think of. Like Harry Truman. Or gallbladder surgery. Or the infield-fly rule. And, if none of that works, there's still the cold shower.

Just because you're wearing dancing shoes doesn't necessarily mean you want to dance. And just because a woman isn't wearing underwear doesn't necessarily mean she is there for the taking.

Abernathy Did the Write Thing

I was surprised that some people were surprised, even outraged, about the Reverend Ralph David Abernathy's mentioning that Dr. Martin Luther King, Jr., often gave in to sexual temptations.

The Reverend Abernathy, a former aide to Dr. King during the civil rights movement, has written an autobiography titled *And the Walls Came Tumbling Down.* In it, he reveals Dr. King even had separate encounters with two women and an argument with another the night before he was murdered in Memphis.

There were plenty of rumors around, even before Dr. King was killed, that he was somewhat of a ladies' man, but I don't understand what all the fuss is about.

Another Atlanta minister has asked his congregation to "do the right thing" and boycott the Reverend Abernathy's book.

There are several reasons that's a dingbat of an idea.

First, when one looks back through the history of our country, many of our finest leaders were, well, bad to fool around with women.

We all know about George Washington, the John Tower of the eighteenth century.

And what about Thomas Jefferson? All the slave girls talked about him.

Ever notice that smug look on Thomas Jefferson's face in history books? You can look at a man like that and tell he's been up to something.

And speaking of Tower again, that's exactly what cost him a spot in the Bush Cabinet.

A friend of mine put it this way, "He just *looks* guilty."

President Grover Cleveland supposedly fathered an illegitimate child. FDR had a mistress. So did Eisenhower. And John Kennedy? When did the man have time to be president?

He probably could have taught Gary Hart, not to mention Rob Lowe, a thing or two. Jimmy Carter even thought about it.

And we know about certain men of the cloth, too. Jimmy Swaggart liked to watch prostitutes do unmentionable things, and if we knew what-all Jim Bakker actually did, we probably wouldn't believe it.

I'm not going to try any Oral Roberts lines here, but where did a first name like that actually come from?

Two: Just because Martin Luther King, Jr., might have had a healthy sexual appetite, it certainly shouldn't diminish anything he accomplished.

The man changed the world. Changed it forever. And did he force any of these women to have sex with him?

Apparently not. They offered. He accepted. That sort of thing has been going on for a long time and likely won't stop any time soon and let us most fervently hope not.

Third, I think it took some guts on the part of Ralph David Abernathy to include Dr. Martin Luther King's sexual escapades in his book.

At one time, the two men obviously were close. And there were King's survivors to consider. And the author could likely have forecast a cry for a boycott, a favorite tool of the civil rights movement.

But more than any allegiances he might have had, and regardless of who might be embarrassed by some of the book's text, the Reverend Abernathy owes the world his memories, and he obviously realized that.

He knew he had sat in on history and had to tell what he had seen and heard. To have done otherwise would have been to gloss over one of the most incredible periods and one of the most incredible men of the century.

What's left to do now is defend Ralph David Abernathy and his right to put what he pleased in his autobiography, to understand the favor he has done all of us who want the inside story on people and events that affect our lives profoundly, and to ignore any dingbat who chirps about a boycott.

Do the right thing, indeed.

The Debt Generation

Donald Trump owes $30 billion. I read that in the papers.

Thirty billion big ones. The only other place you might find that many zeros is at a professional wrestling match.

But Trump, in an incredibly excessive way, is merely an example of how my generation looks at money in comparison to the way our parents did.

If my mother had been put in charge of the nation's budget, there never would have been a deficit.

She had some basic rules when it came to money:

1. Spend the least possible amount of what you have and save the rest.
2. If you have to borrow to pay for it, you can get by without it.
3. The secret to having peace of mind is not owing a single penny.

Our parents took a lot of pride in being debtless. To owe was a sign of weakness of character to them.

A friend my age said, "My father was proudest of the fact everything he owned was paid for. I used to tell him, "But you don't have very much."

"He would always say, 'But what little I have nobody can take away. Can you say that?' I couldn't."

As an adult, I never mentioned my finances around my mother. She would have been astounded at what baby boomers have been able to earn.

But she would have been deeply distressed by the debt I have incurred.

I once spent nearly six times what it cost my mother and stepfather to build a new house in 1956 for an automobile, which I financed, of course.

I borrowed more money from the bank to pay for my house than my mother made in her career as a schoolteacher.

But that is how my generation found the good life.

We borrow, and it doesn't bother us to owe up the wazoo.

I worked with a guy in the seventies who was telling me about a letter he got from one of his creditors.

"They're mad about the fact I missed a payment," he said.

"The way I pay my bills is, I put them all in a hat. Then I reach into the hat without looking and pull out a bill.

"I keep doing that until I'm out of money. There are always a few bills left in the hat, but at least everybody I owe has the same chance of being pulled out of the hat.

"I wrote the people back and told them if they sent me another nasty letter, I wouldn't even put them in the hat anymore."

Why is my generation so willing to go into the Black Hole of Indebtedness when our parents were so afraid of it?

We never lived through a depression, for one thing. We grew up with television, for another. Would I really have wanted a Cadillac someday if I hadn't seen them being given away on *The $64,000 Question?*

Our parents sent us to college in droves. The more education we got, the more earning power we got, and the more money we made, the more we developed the attitude "It's only money. I'll make some more tomorrow."

If Donald Trump can go down, how about the rest of us? Haven't we all been guilty of our own little episodes of extravagance and greed?

How safe are we from the wolf at the door?

Our frugal, save-for-a-rainy-day parents said things like, "Never borrow from Peter to pay Paul."

The Debt Generation sports bumper stickers that say, "He who dies with the most toys wins."

That's sad.

Devilish Turn of Events for Hitler

The Devil called Hitler into his air-conditioned office in Hell.

"Nice, huh?" smiled the Devil.

Hitler, soaked in sweat from another day in the steaming, blistering heat of his just reward, nodded weakly.

"But don't get used to it," the Devil warned. "As soon as I'm through with you, it's back to upside down in the dung pit."

Again, Hitler nodded. The dung pit was Hell's Who's Who, a sort of Hall of Infamy for history's Really Nasty Boys.

Besides Hitler, the lineup included the Ayatollah Khomeini, Joe Stalin, Attila the Hun, Jack the Ripper, and the advertising executives who came up with the phrase "new and improved."

"I know you've been out of touch for forty-five years," the Devil went on, "but I think you'll get a kick out of what's going on upstairs."

Hitler's mustache twitched with anticipation.

"First of all," said the Devil, "your beloved Fatherland is back."

"But that can't be," said Hitler. "I heard the Allies split us up after the war so that we would be too weak to cause the world any more trouble."

"That's true, *mein Führer*," mocked the Devil. "But now East Germany and West Germany are reunifying and are on the verge of becoming THE dominant force in Europe again."

"But how did this happen?" asked an amazed Hitler. "Why didn't the Soviet Union put a stop to such a thing?"

"Because," said the Devil, "the Soviet Union is up to its babushka in its own troubles. The Soviet economy is a joke. Communism is in big trouble, and Eastern bloc nations are lifting themselves from under the weakened Soviet thumb."

"I can't wait to tell Joe back at the dung pit," laughed Hitler.

He continued: "But what about the British and the Americans? They didn't see the threat of a return of a unified, powerful Germany?"

"Are you serious?" asked the Devil. "They're too busy with their own problems, too. Unemployment is rampant in Britain, and the Americans owe everybody and his brother-in-law."

Hitler, elated, did a jig step. "*Wunderbar*, the Fatherland is back in business," he exclaimed.

"So is Japan," said the Devil.

"But the rumor over at the pit was the Americans nuked the Japanese off the map in '45," said Hitler.

"They did," said the Devil. "But you know the Japanese. They're as strong and rich as ever."

"Do they have any plans for another sneak attack on the Americans?" asked Hitler, licking his chops.

"No," answered the Devil. "They've got a new plan. They're buying the United States building by building, golf course by golf course."

"Let me see if I have all this straight," said Hitler to the Devil.

"Deutschland is being reunified and is once again emerging as a world power, and the Japanese are back in clover.

"And the Soviet Union is belly-up, and the British still haven't learned a thing, and the Americans can't pay their bills."

"That's about it," said the Devil.

"I don't guess there's any possibility I could . . ." began Hitler, before being interrupted by the Devil.

"Forget it," he said to Hitler. "You had your chance."

Hitler, severely disappointed he wasn't going to get another opportunity at trying to take over the world, cursed under his breath and was returned to the dung pit.

"Dang," said the Devil a few moments later. "I forgot to tell him about the skinheads."

Mr. Smith Goes to Neil Bush

A wino walks into the Silverado Savings and Loan and says to the next available teller, "I want some money."

"You want to cash a check?" the teller asks.

"No," says the wino. "I don't have any money, and I want some."

"Then it's a loan you're after," replies the teller. "You would need to see Mr. Bush about that."

The wino is directed to Miss Hullingsworth, Mr. Bush's secretary. Mr. Bush is director of Silverado Savings and Loan.

"Go right in," says a smiling Miss Hullingsworth.

"You Bush?" the wino asks.

"I prefer you call me Neil."

"I want some money."

"Then it's a loan you're after. You have come to the right place. What do you need this money for?"

"Wine."

"You're going to start a winery. Fantastic. I'm sort of a wine lover myself. The Chablis Grand Cru I had at dinner last evening was arrogant but certainly not offensive. Is that a favorite of yours, too?"

"I had a pint of Thunderbird for breakfast."

"Wine with breakfast? Interesting. How much do you need to start your winery?"

"I'm not starting no winery. I just need some money to buy some more Thunderbird."

"Oh, you're a wine collector. What other wines are you interested in?"

"Ripple. MD 20-20, Wild Russian Vonya. Mennen Skin Bracer, in a pinch."

"I'll need some information. Just routine. Your name?"

"Give me a minute."

"Take all the time you need."

"It's Grover. But they call me 'Shaky.' "

"How did you get a nickname like that?"

"Look at my hands."

"Wow. That's some case of Saint Vitus' dance. And your last name?"

"I can't remember."

"That's okay. We'll give you one. Let's call you 'Mr. Smith' then. And your address?"

"Alley next to the pool hall, third cardboard box on the left."

"Occupation?"

"I was a brain surgeon before the malpractice suit."

"Married?"

"She left me when I went broke."

"And exactly how much money do you need?"

"How's a hundred?"

"Can do. One hundred thousand dollars. What the hell. Let's

make it two hundred thousand. You never know if you might need a little extra. Now, Mr. Smith, what sort of collateral do you have?"

"None."

"No collateral? Who's worried about details? Now if you will just take this form up to the next available teller, you can get your loan."

"Can I have it in cash?"

"Of course you can. At Silverado, we always aim to please. Your payments, by the way, will be fourteen-hundred-fifty dollars a month.

"I gotta pay this back?"

"Don't worry about it now. Just drop back by in a month or so and we'll talk about it then."

"Thanks, Neil."

"It was my pleasure, Mr. Smith. Miss Hullingsworth, please get my father on the phone. He's late sending my allowance again."

Zeroing In on a Japanese Buy-out

My friend Rigsby, the paranoid schizophrenic, was voicing his concern about the visit of Japanese prime minister Toshiki Kaifu to Atlanta.

"What's your problem with Prime Minister Kaifu?" I asked him.

"Ever since he arrived in town, all he's done is smile, I saw him on television," said Rigsby.

"Why would you be concerned about his smiling?"

"Did you see the movie *Tora! Tora! Tora!?*" Rigsby asked me.

"Sure I saw it," I said. "It was about the Japanese sneak attack on Pearl Harbor."

"And remember when the Japanese pilots realized they had, indeed, pulled off a sneak attack? They smiled."

"So?"

"And do you remember those World War Two movies where the Japanese fighter pilot gets on his radio and talks to the American pilot he has in his gunsights?"

"I've seen that, yes."

"The Japanese pilot always says, 'I was educated at UCLA, Yankee dog, Brooklyn Dodger. Now, you die.'"

"That's vaguely familiar."

"Well, the Japanese pilot is smiling the whole time."

"Let me see if I'm reading you correctly," I said to Rigsby. "You think when you see a Japanese person smiling, it means they're up to something."

"You've got it."

"So what are you afraid of Mr. Kaifu for? Do you think he's planning a sneak attack on Atlanta?"

"Worse," said Rigsby. "I'm afraid he's going to figure out a way to buy it."

"The whole town?"

"It could happen," said Rigsby. "The Japanese already have gotten a head start. They've bought office buildings and a golf course in Atlanta. Georgia is second only to California in the number of Japanese investments."

"So you see a dangerous trend?"

"I do," said Rigsby. "First, they buy up office buildings and golf courses, then they get their hands on hotels and apartment buildings.

"Next comes auto dealerships and pancake houses. Then, Kentucky Fried Chicken franchises and liquor stores. Then they take over places that sell Oriental rugs because they figure the rugs are theirs in the first place.

"After that, movie theaters and hardware stores. All you'll be able to see are martial-arts movies where the sound doesn't match the actors' mouths, and every time you buy a screwdriver, you'll just be adding to the Japanese wealth. Before you know it, they'll own the airport, the governor's mansion, the newspaper, all the radio and television stations, the rights to *Gone With the Wind* and Coca-Cola, and we'll be foreigners in our own city."

"Coke would never sell to the Japanese," I said.

"You haven't heard what the Japanese are offering," said Rigsby.

I certainly wasn't taking Rigsby seriously, but I did continue to humor him.

"Is there anything in Atlanta, then, the Japanese won't try to buy?"

"Only two things," he answered. "The Braves and the Falcons."

"Why not?"

"I may not trust the Japanese," said Rigsby, "but I never said they weren't smart."

Street Gangs with Gunning Little Ways

City officials said they hoped people wouldn't be frightened away from the Atlanta mall because there was a gang rumble in the vicinity and a man was shot dead.

Of course we won't. Just because the Drips and Cruds were

playing war games near the mall and a guy got blown away, why should we be afraid to leave our homes and our alarm systems to go to the mall and visit a real crime scene?

Beats watching the Braves.

Mayor Maynard Jackson, in a rare showing of good sense, wants the police to arrest anybody suspected of being involved in a gang, since gangs are known for their drug dealings and their penchant for violence.

So, reasoned the mayor, if we rounded up gang members, the city's streets and the mall might be a lot safer.

But the American Civil Liberties Union wouldn't hear of that.

"Just because you belong to a gang," an ACLU spokesliberal said, "doesn't give the police the right to arrest you."

We're not talking about the Boy Scouts here. We're talking about dangerous young men with guns and a tendency toward pack mentality. They like to wear their own colors.

If policemen see the colors on the street, they at least should have the right to see if anybody's packing AK-47s, bazookas, or surface-to-air missiles—some of the preferred weapons of gangs that can, in fact, shoot straight.

But that probably wouldn't stand up in court, so I've got another idea.

We let the gangs fight it out in Atlanta Stadium and sell tickets. Which would you rather watch: the Braves strand another fifteen base runners or the Mad Dogs and the Killer Bees shoot it out?

We flock to see violent movies. I went to see *Lethal Weapon II*, and 416 people got shot while they were still running the credits.

Promoters would put up protective shields at the stadium so paying customers wouldn't get shot. Proceeds from the events could go to help families of innocents killed in gang violence.

We might even televise such events.

"Hello again, everybody. This is Skip Caray with another exciting night of *Gang Shoot-out*.

"Tonight, it's the Brutes against the Really Really Bad Boys. I'll be back for the starting lineups, but first this word from the Grim Reaper Funeral Home and Death Knell Hospital, featuring the latest in emergency room techniques."

You don't think the wrestling fans would flock to see something like that?

"Hey, look, Harold, them's real bullets! That's real blood!"

Okay, I know you can't really do that. Too barbaric, too much like the Roman Games.

But allow me the fantasy. The gangs eventually kill each other off in the stadium rather than on the streets, where a visitor to the mall or a baby in a crib catches a stray bullet.

Colors. Have a nice funeral.

Movie Casting, Japanese Style

American filmgoers are concerned—and rightly so— about the fact that the Japanese have just about bought up Hollywood as a part of their never-ending shopping spree in this country.

Another movie studio fell into Japanese hands the other day, and the question becomes, What effect will this have on the sort of movies we will be seeing in the future, and will we have to take off our shoes when we go to the theater?

First, we must deal with the issue of what sort of movies the Japanese have done in the past.

For example, the Japanese like to make movies that feature very large things that enjoy devouring entire cities.

How often have you not been able to sleep and turned on the

tube at 3:00 A.M. to see a lizard with an obvious gland disorder gobbling up Japanese real estate, not to mention a couple hundred thousand citizens who were unlucky enough to be standing on it?

Can we expect *Rocky XII* where Sylvester Stallone meets Godzilla in a fifteen-rounder?

"Wearing orange trunks and weighing twenty-seven thousand tons, the challenger, Kid God-ziiiiil-la!"

The positive side of this, of course, is Godzilla will probably eat Sylvester Stallone and the entire cast sometime during the early rounds, and we will finally have absolutely, positively seen the last *Rocky*.

And what of future World War II movies? The Japanese have a lot of revenge to get here.

My favorite World War II movie is *Tora! Tora! Tora!*, which is Japanese for "Bombs Away, Takushi, we've caught 'em with their pants down."

That movie is all about the surprise attack on Pearl Harbor by the Japanese. They still win big at Pearl in the movie, but the script does imply at the end what eventually happened: that the residents of Hiroshima and Nagasaki regretted that December 7, 1941, ever happened.

Will *Tora! Tora! Tora! II* show the Japanese leaving Pearl Harbor and not slowing down until the outskirts of Indianapolis?

And what of the way the Japanese soldier has always been depicted on the American screen?

He's always a scrawny little guy wearing a funny hat with thick eyeglasses and protruding teeth. What did we think, every brave Nippon warrior had bad eyesight and sucked his thumb until he was twenty-one?

In a Japanese remake of *Guadalcanal Diary* will their soldiers wear contacts, get their teeth fixed, and wear something from the latest Ralph Lauren combat collection?

Then there's the Japanese interest in movies that feature the martial arts.

In a remake of *Gone With the Wind* will Danny Glover as

Rhett (what do the Japanese know about the Civil War?) bid his famous "Frankly, my dear, I don't give a damn" farewell to Scarlett—played by the talented Japanese actress Kimono Lisa— by screaming "Kaaaaa-chinga!" and then kick her in the mouth?

The most concern I have, however, is will the new Japanese-owned studios be able to make movies where the mouths of the actors and actresses correspond with the words coming out of them?

You're watching another Japanese martial-arts movie and one guy says to another, "I'm going to do some serious damage to your hind parts," but his mouth is about a beat ahead of the words and seems to be saying instead, "My, but don't you look lovely this evening?"

Some may say I am showing my xenophobia here (the fear of foreigners or anybody named Xeno), but isn't it time we start wondering if our great nation isn't holding a going-out-of business sale?

Or, put better, when, oh when, will all this yen? (I'm sorry I just couldn't stop myself).

AT HOME

Dan Ackroyd trying to do a Southern accent in *Driving Miss Daisy* is like me trying to sing like Pavarotti. (I can do a little Willie Nelson, however.)

Future Olympic Games Develop Growing Paynes

A preview of Atlanta's upcoming road to the 1996 Olympic Games.

• 1991: Atlanta Mayor Maynard Jackson and Billy Payne, who organized the effort to bring the Games to Atlanta, have a serious falling-out over which one can answer questions first at Olympic press conferences.

The mayor says, "I'm the oldest." But Payne says, "You're also the fattest, but I did all the work."

Civil rights leader Hosea Williams, gets into the fray and says he'll be glad to run the Olympics, if he is given a new Lincoln Town Car and diplomatic immunity from traffic tickets.

Realizing what a mistake that would be, the mayor and Payne make up and vow to restore harmony to the Atlanta Olympic planning team.

The mayor will answer first at press conferences, but Payne will get the aisle seat when the two fly on Olympic business.

A few weeks later, residents of the area near the site of the new Olympic stadium block bulldozers from clearing the area for construction.

The residents claim building the stadium will be a nuisance to them.

Mayor Jackson arrives and tries to end the tension. In the confusion, he is run over by one of the bulldozers.

The protesters finally disperse and agree to the construction when the mayor, unharmed but noticeably flat, promises them the stadium parking concession with full price-gouging rights.

A couple of months later, construction begins on the stadium, but the mayor is still complaining about difficulty in breathing due to the fact the bottom half of his nose is covering his mouth after the unfortunate accident with the bulldozer.

• 1992: The city council votes itself all the tickets it wants for the '96 games, not to mention a limo to each event, a fifteen-thousand-dollar raise, and an unlimited expense account to entertain foreign dignitaries.

Said a city council person who asked not to be identified: "Do we have a great political system or what?"

Residents in the area continue to protest construction of an Olympic tennis facility in their neighborhood.

The tennis site is then moved to Forsyth County. Hosea Williams announces he will return to the county and will drive through it this time, rather than march, if the stadium isn't named after him.

Fearing for their lives, Forsyth officials convince the Olympic Committee to okay the Hosea Williams Olympic Tennis Stadium and also offer him an honorary membership in the local chapter of Ducks Unlimited.

• 1993: Billy Payne says all the politics involved in Olympics has "made me sick" and says he is "washing my hands of the entire mess."

Aware of the fact that Mayor Jackson continues to seek an even larger role in the Olympics, Payne suggests His Rotundity participate in the Olympics in a newly created event, Javelin Catching.

Asked about his future plans, Payne said he may seek to bring the Indianapolis 500 to Atlanta. Georgia governor Zell Miller announces he will allow Olympic equestrian events to be held in the yard of the governor's mansion.

"But what about the smell?" the governor is asked.

"I'm used to it," he said, referring to his many years of service in the state capital.

· 1994: Billy Payne wins the new Georgia lottery and moves to Australia.

· 1995: Two Atlanta gangs, the Crips and Bloods, wipe each other out in an automatic-weapons battle, reinforcing Atlanta's reputation as "Murder Capital, USA."

Mayor Jackson holds a press conference to deny Atlanta is unsafe for Olympic visitors.

"Any city has a few bad apples," said the mayor, crouching behind his desk.

Iraq, meanwhile, announced it will boycott the 1996 Games and invade Scandinavia instead.

No More for Moreland

Now here's my little hometown of Moreland, forty miles south and fifty years from Atlanta. It is still a village of maybe four hundred, and it still doesn't have a traffic light and it doesn't want one.

Oh, there's been a little progress since I left dear Moreland nearly thirty years ago.

There's a new brick post office, for instance, that succeeds the old wooden one.

Somebody even built a couple of tennis courts in Moreland, and there actually is a Moreland exit sign on Interstate 85 that missed my hometown by three miles to the north.

Still, after all these years, Moreland has remained a quiet little blip on the map, a haven for those who have no use for city lights.

So you can judge just how shocked I was after reading a letter I received from Alan E. Thomas, who works in Atlanta.

Alan E. Thomas wrote to tell me that he and his wife have spent the last three years constructing a new farm home in Moreland.

"Like so many others," he wrote, "we're leaving city life and beginning to experience the wonders of the country.

"At night, we can step out on the deck and actually see stars again, and hear the crickets, frogs, and whippoorwills and spot herds of deer crossing from one tree cluster to another."

Ah, such splendor. Such peace.

But Alan E. Thomas and his wife and other Moreland citizens suddenly are faced with a problem I never thought could happen there.

Jet noise.

I can recall the noise of freight trains rumbling through Moreland nights during my childhood, and once a local turkey farmer got upset because he said the Baptist church's chimes made his turkeys nervous, but jet noise?

Alan E. Thomas writes that the Coweta County Airport Authority wants to expand its little facility, which sits just on the outskirts of Moreland, so it can accommodate corporate jets. Corporate jets?

I doubt any corporate jets would land there to do any business in Moreland. There is the expanding county seat of Newnan nearby, but any corporate jets with business in Newnan simply could land at Hartsfield. It's only twenty-five miles away.

Alan E. Thomas wants to be able to continue hearing the rural night sounds and not have them drowned out by the menacing roar of a jet engine.

He and others have suggested a new airport be built somewhere else. But the Airport Authority has explained the Federal Aviation Administration will grant funds for a runway extension, but not for a completely new airport.

Governmental red tape and bureaucratic bumfuzzle strike again.

Mr. Thomas has suggested I become an ally in the fight against jet noise in Moreland, and I assure him he now can count me on his side.

Moreland and Newnan need a place for jets to take off and land like they need a disco, and rural nights should still belong to the crickets, frogs, and whippoorwills.

Fight like hell, my fellow Morelanders, and save the sacred quiet.

Once that's lost, God forbid, a traffic light is sure to follow.

Can Scholars Fill the Void?

ATHENS, GA.—I introduced myself to the studious-looking, bespectacled young man coming out of class on the University of Georgia campus the other morning.

I had remained in Athens after attending Saturday's Ole Miss–Georgia football game, which Georgia lost.

Many Bulldog fans are despondent because of Georgia's current 3–3 record, and the fact the Bulldogs have fallen from the circle of college football's elite.

Some of the football problems can be directly attributed to the fact that the university administration, led by President Charles Knapp and many forward-thinking members of the faculty, has determined Georgia should upgrade its academics and become, as one faculty source told me, "Harvard on the Oconee." (The reference is to the Oconee River, which flows through Athens, and was once the site of many a spirited rowing match, until after the Jan Kemp trial when all the Bulldog oarsmen flunked out of school.)

Georgia's increased academic requirements of athletes, more stringent than most of its competitors', also have cost the football team its defensive line. There's also a rumor another player is in academic hot water for being caught gazing out a window during his botany professor's brilliant lecture on stamens and pistils. (Not the rock group of the same name.)

So what I was doing introducing myself to the young man was trying to find a brilliant student who would make Georgia football fans forget we don't have a quarterback or a defense, but at least we could be proud of academic achievement instead.

The young man said he was Arnold Snedgemeyer, III, of the West Paces Ferry Snedgemeyers of Atlanta.

"So how did you do in class today?" I asked him.

"Aced my history test," he said.

"How 'bout them Dawgs!" I yelled.

"Pul-leeze," the young man replied. "Besides, for someone who made a perfect score on his SAT, it was a piece of cake."

"With a perfect score on your SAT, you could have gone anywhere to college. Why did you choose Georgia?"

"Certainly I wouldn't have back when Georgia was allowing all those public-school ninnies from those atrocious little towns outside Atlanta to enroll. Dad would never have stood for it," Arnold explained.

"So," I went on, "you don't think students who don't have your brainpower should be admitted to their state university?"

"What? And have us gifted be guilty by association? That's absurd. Where did you go to school, Auburn?"

"As a matter of fact," I said, "I'm a Georgia graduate."

"No doubt you were here in the Dark Ages," sneered Arnold.

"Well, I must admit I didn't make exactly a perfect score on my SAT," I said.

"That much I presumed," Arnold sneered once more.

"Arnold," I pressed on, ignoring his elitist remarks, "how big are you?"

"I'm five-eight, one hundred thirty pounds without my glasses. Why do you ask?"

"Well, when we used to sign a good football player, the fans always wanted to know his size. I guess I'm just reminiscing."

"Whatever, Old Sport," said Arnold. "I'm off to chemistry. Big test today. *Au revoir.*"

Before I left the campus, I walked back and gazed at Sanford Stadium where once we cheered for Stanfill and Belue and Walker and Scott and Johnson and Ol' Moonpie Wilson and Cowboy Parrish.

But now, I suppose, we must look to the Arnold Snedgemeyers to fill their void.

Is it any wonder, then, there was a bumpersticker at Saturday's game that read, "We've been 'Kemp-Knapped.' "

Get Yourself Another Driver, Miss Daisy

"Hoke, drive me to the Piggly Wiggly. I need to pick up some groceries."

"Nome, Miss Daisy, I don't think we should leave the house."

"What kind of foolishness is that, Hoke?"

"Didn't you know, Miss Daisy, that Atlanta has the highest crime rate of any large city in the country?"

"Where did you get such notions as that, Hoke?"

"It was in the paper, Miss Daisy. According to FBI statistics, Atlanta ranks number one in crime."

"That's silly, Hoke. Everybody knows that New York City has the highest crime rate. My son, Boolie, went there once, and somebody broke into his hotel room and stole his socks and underwear and he was wearing them at the time."

"Nome, Miss Daisy. New York was way yonder behind Atlanta in crime."

"Well, where was Detroit? I had a cousin who went to Detroit and somebody snatched a purse in front of the Pontchartrain Hotel."

"Detroit was fourth, Miss Daisy."

"That's nonsense, Hoke. Atlanta is a kind, genteel Southern city. I've never heard of anyone getting their purse snatched here."

"Yessum, Miss Daisy. My cousin was walking down Peachtree Street, and somebody snatched her purse and hit her in the head to boot. In broad daylight, Miss Daisy, and she knows kung fu."

"That nice Chinese man who works for the Alexanders?"

"Nome, Miss Daisy. Kung fu is a martial art. Didn't do my cousin no good to know it, though. The thief knew tire tool."

"Hoke, I have lived in Atlanta my entire life, and we do not have a serious crime problem here. I don't know a single person who has been murdered."

"That's because you live in this rich, white neighborhood, Miss Daisy. Everybody up here dies from old age and colon cancer. In my neighborhood we don't need no alarm clocks. The ambulance wakes us up in the morning going to pick up another dead body."

"Well, why don't you move out from down there, Hoke?"

"And move up here next to you, Miss Daisy? I'd have to rob a bank to get that kind of money, and you got to stand in line to rob a bank in Atlanta."

"It doesn't matter, Hoke. I still must go to the Piggly Wiggly. If you won't drive me, I'll take a streetcar. I always took a streetcar when I was a girl."

"That was sixty-five years ago, Miss Daisy. They done put extra drivers on the streetcars now to ride shotgun."

"I don't care, Hoke. Now I insist you go get the Hudson and take me to the Piggly Wiggly."

"Don't have the Hudson no more, Miss Daisy."

"What happened to it?"

"Your son traded it in for a Wells Fargo truck, Miss Daisy. You can't take no chances in Atlanta anymore."

"Well, why don't city officials do something about the crime problem in Atlanta?"

"They say they're working on it, Miss Daisy. But that them statistics is a lie."

"What do you think, Hoke?"

"I think I'm moving to Detroit, Miss Daisy. Here's the keys to the Wells Fargo truck. The shotgun's under the seat."

Sore Losers

Sports columnist for the *Atlanta Constitution* Steve Hummer has been keeping up with what some of his colleagues from around the nation are saying about Atlanta and the fact it will host the 1996 Olympic Games.

He quoted a guy from Baltimore as typing, "Choosing between Athens and Atlanta seems simple enough. Athens is called the Birthplace of Western Civilization. Atlanta gave us Lester Maddox."

A person from Santa Clara, California, vomited, "I thought Atlanta was Spartanburg with skyscrapers."

And then:

". . . Atlanta, no matter how tall it is, how big or congested, it is still The South. It is not cosmopolitan by anyone's definition."

There were similar comments from the *Los Angeles Times* and *The Washington Post*. There was this from Scott Ostler of *The National*:

". . . Does this mean pro wrestling will be an Olympic sport?"

You don't know what *The National* is? Not many people do, either, but, for the record, it's a forgettable daily sports tabloid they sell in cosmopolitan places like New York for something to read between subway murders and racial skirmishes.

On journalism's weather radar screen, *The National* would turn up as a small blip that would be dismissed by the weatherman thusly: "Don't pay any attention to this, it's only ground clutter."

Hummer put Baltimore in its place, pointing out it couldn't even keep its pro-football team from moving to Indianapolis, once referred to as a cornfield with lights.

Is Santa Rosa any relation to Santa Claus? Is L.A. still on the continent, or has it finally dropped off into the Pacific?

Washington? If they held the Olympics in Washington, would Mayor Nose Candy light his pipe on the Olympic flame?

Hacks and flacks. Why aren't these people writing about something at which they are experts, such as how to get the team PR guy to pick up the bar tab?

Or why not dissertations on who's going to win the baseball play-offs or mindless drivel on this year's chances for the Utah Jazz?

Where did they want the 1996 Games? In Athens?

I've been to Athens. Twice. The airport's a barn. It's little New York with older ruins.

How about Belgrade? Do the Slavs mind if you're wearing a white belt to match your shoes, the preferred press-box attire?

How about Manchester? Maybe a soccer riot will break out and a few hundred people will get trampled. But how many of these ninnies could cover a story more complicated than a guy jumping over a stick?

Yes, Atlanta is still The South, which just happens to be The Place to Be.

Atlanta shocked the world. Atlanta went for the gold and got it.

While cities like New York and Boston and Washington have moved backward, Atlanta has never looked anywhere but straight ahead.

And it has left the real losersvilles like Baltimore to pout in the squalor of their own jealously and ignorance.

By God.

The Man Who Put Zest in Sex

A man walked up to me in a public setting recently and asked, "Is it true the University of Georgia is installing Astroturf at the football stadium to stop the cheerleaders from grazing?"

People who know of my fierce loyalty to my alma mater often tell me jokes like that. But I'm always prepared to retaliate.

The man said he was a Clemson graduate, so I asked him, "Do you know the only place you can buy push-up bras for pigs?"

He didn't.

I said, "Frederick's of Clemson."

The very next day I was reading the paper and read where Frederick, his own self, was dead. He was Frederick Mellinger.

In 1946, he started his Frederick's of Hollywood mail-order

lingerie business, which eventually would sell enough sexy underwear for women to keep Madonna half-naked on stage for four thousand years without having to wear the same outfit twice.

Frederick's of Hollywood shops would open in places like shopping malls. Frederick's of Hollywood storefronts became the most popular place for men to window-shop at a mall, far outdistancing their previous favorite, the cute puppies in the window of the pet store.

I fell in love with a Frederick's manikin or two myself. One wore a blond wig and she was there bedecked for the bedroom in scandalous scanties, a sight much more interesting than watching two beagle puppies step in their water bowls.

Another was a raven-haired beauty in a red peekaboo. One night, I dreamed I was looking at her in Frederick's and she came to life right before my eyes.

I was arrested by mall security, however, when I chased her all the way through the garden-supply department at Sears. I was over by the zinnia seeds, completely out of breath, when they nabbed me.

I've also done my share of shopping at Frederick's. That's where I went to buy my first wife a gift on our second anniversary.

"May I help you with something?" a saleswoman asked.

"Just browsing, thanks," I said.

Two hours later I was pretty much browsed out, not to mention covered in perspiration and experiencing episodes of heart palpitations. Browsing at Frederick's of Hollywood lingerie conjured so many thrilling possibilities.

I settled on a nightie for my wife. Was it small? I carried it out of there in my wallet.

When my wife saw what I had bought her, she said, "Pervert."

My first wife was an old-fashioned girl. Whenever we decided to make love with the lights on, she would pull all the window shades and put a For Sale sign in our front yard.

Frederick Mellinger was one of the first people in this country to realize sex would sell in a big way.

But he should not be remembered as some soft-porn sleazo. He did us a favor. He put a little zest in American bedrooms, and a good time was had by all.

I made up the part about my first wife calling me a pervert. She did, in fact, put on the Frederick's nightie, and she looked sexier than a Clemson cheerleader wearing nothing on beneath her overalls.

Atlanta's Sex Scene

Look what's happened to that grand ol' gal of the South, Atlanta.

She's become a sexpot.

She's Hollywood East. She's where it's happening, sexually speaking.

I'm not certain when all this started. I'd guess you'd go all the way back to Scarlett O'Hara.

Let's face it, she was hot. I still think Ashley probably gave in to her advances at least a couple of times, and she probably was involved with the Tarleton twins, too. Maybe even at the same time. A *ménage à Tara.*

Now, we zoom to modern times. The last great sex scandal of the eighties took place in Atlanta.

Rob Lowe. The sixteen-year-old girl. "Sexiest Hotel Room Videos" and all that.

A political party (the one besides the Republicans, I forget the exact name) decides to hold its national convention in Atlanta, and the big story is Rob Lowe and sex, not Michael What's-his-name and politics.

And then there is the mysterious case of the sixteen thousand condoms (unused, I presume) being stolen from Atlanta's Grady Hospital.

That really happened. As far as I know, the culprit or culprits have not been fetched, but is Rob Lowe tied into this in any way?

The man obviously has the sexual appetite of a West Texas jackrabbit.

Steve Garvey, the Rob Lowe of baseball, has a fling with an Atlanta woman during all the sexual mess he got into.

And Rankin Smith, Jr., president of the Atlanta Falcons, gets hit with a paternity suit by a woman who claims he fathered not one, but two, of her babies.

No wonder the Falcons have been so bad. When did Junior have time to run the team?

Now, the latest: Atlanta Catholic archbishop Eugene A. Marino has been sexually linked with a twenty-seven-year-old looker, who claims he exploited her when she came to him for counsel regarding sexual abuse by another priest.

Isn't this a spicy little number? Let's call it "Celibate Is Irrelevant," or, "It Sure Gets Hot Under the Collar in the Summertime."

Personally, I enjoy a good sex scandal occasionally, but Atlanta has had a veritable buffet of them.

Is it in the drinking water? Is it the steamy nights with all that humidity?

Is there a connection with the fact our sports teams are always so lousy?

Does Jane Fonda, rumored to be more than just friends with Ted Turner, have anything to do with any of this?

What does the pope have to say? Do any of the participants in Atlanta's sex scene sleep with a trumpet?

Was Scarlett, if the truth be known, actually a nympho who

slept with a third or so of the entire Confederate Army? How long would sixteen thousand condoms last her?

Did anybody ever realize just how much fun priesthood could be?

I wish I had some answers for these questions, but I don't. I also don't think there is a shred of truth to the rumor that Rhett Butler was actually bisexual and walked out on Scarlett rather than tell her of his true feelings for a certain young Union lieutenant he met at a gay bar Sherman missed.

Georgia Tech, Georgia on My Mind

I suppose I could just go run under a log and hide and allow this Georgia Tech football thing to cool down, but, unlike my Yellow Jacket friends think, I am a man of principle.

Here I am in the midst of the worst Georgia football season since George and Barbara were just dating, but I can't allow that to interfere with my duty to congratulate Tech for its astounding victory over top-ranked Virginia last Saturday.

What a game!

The Jackets came back and likely will win their first conference title of any kind (I read this in another paper) since 1952.

I hope Georgia's high priests of academia, who think a successful football season is based on how many players flunk out of school, saw the game.

Virginia and Georgia Tech, two institutions with pristine academic images, didn't get on national television playing the Game of the Day without a little help from their administrations.

There is absolutely nothing wrong, in my mind, with recruiting young athletes, and if they can't all be rocket scientists, then find something they can handle.

General Studies. American Studies. Sports Management. Rhetoric. Mechanics and Tow Truck Engineering. It doesn't matter.

Until every school agrees all athletes must make 1200 on their SATs and be able to understand Goethe, schools that don't bend here and there are destined to 4–7 records and no chance at the glory.

Perhaps empty seats and dwindling alumni contributions will strike a chord, even if these words won't.

Tech's team is big, strong, and fast. Would any Tech fan alive Saturday give up the precious victory over Virginia because the school will give a kid who didn't exactly tear up his college boards a chance to play and stay in school?

That is to be commended, not condemned. This should not be an elitist society. To deny the average student at an institution supported by public funds is an elitist idea.

(Forgive my preaching, but when you're 4–4 and facing Florida, Auburn, and Tech and no bowl, it's enough to make a man take to the pulpit to speak of Doomsday.)

Georgia may have about a one-in-a-hundred chance of upsetting one of its last three opponents. I asked fellow Dawgs which one they would pick if they could have that one.

It's sort of half-and-half between Auburn and Tech.

"We've beaten Florida so much," one said.

I'd take Tech. No doubt the Yellow Jackets will come to Athens 9–0–1, bound for a New Year's Day bowl. How sweet it would be to spoil that trip.

I hope that says to Tech fans how much I respect their team. The tables have turned. It's been Tech wanting to spoil Georgia trips for so many years.

Make no mistake. Georgia will be back. If we have to storm the palace, we will; but we'll be back.

In the meantime Georgia Tech will hog the headlines. The Ramblin' Wreck, what a helluva shape it was in, but no more.

Now, that's about all the goodwill for the event I can stand out of myself for one day.

See you in Athens.

When "Big Mac" Ran Into a Stop Sign

A woman at the Illinois corporate headquarters of McDonald's said the company has now served 75 billion hamburgers.

Some quick arithmetic tells me that is about three hundred hamburgers for every man, woman, and child in America and 2 million for Oprah Winfrey.

But McDonald's is not going to add to that number in Helen, Georgia.

Helen is a little town in the north Georgia mountains with the Alpine theme.

Tourists flock to Helen and spend a lot of money there sightseeing and buying trinkets. I've heard Helen described as "quite quaint."

The town gambled on the Alpine theme in 1968. "Before that," said Cliff Hood of the Helen planning board, "Helen was a ghost town."

A ghost town with dusty streets, vacant saloons, and tumbling tumbleweeds might have brought in tourists, too, if it had a name like Dry Gulch, but whoever heard of a ghost town named after a girl?

McDonald's wanted a crack at some of Helen's tourists, and you know how McDonald's is. You can have mayonnaise only if they say you can have mayonnaise. Make way for the Golden Arches.

But the Helen planning board said McDonald's would have to live by its building and sign restrictions, which include no internally lit signs and only certain colors.

McDonald's at night looks like an airport. They could have put a few McDonald's in the neighborhood and saved the money they spent on lighting Wrigley Field in Chicago and simply used the glow Big Mac puts out.

According to Cliff Hood, McDonald's did agree to forget the golden arches and a lighted road sign. (There apparently was no discussion concerning whether Ronald McDonald would be out front waving cars in.)

And McDonald's agreed to add some additional wood trim. But McDonald's wouldn't budge on its big fluorescent lighted roof beams, which are also a violation of Helen building codes.

"A lot of people staked their life savings on the Alpine theme," said Cliff Hood, "and they didn't want to compromise it."

The end result was Helen refused McDonald's a building permit and told Ronald to go eat those silly shoes he wears.

Helen has a Wendy's because Wendy's agreed to conform to the Alpine motif.

But McDonald's wouldn't, and Helen stuck to its guns.

There ought to be more of that sort of thing. Cities and towns should say more often, "You want to put a building here? Fine, but it better not look like a space station."

There's nothing wrong with quaint. We like quaint. It's why we flock to Europe to take pictures of one another standing in front of a quaint little shop in a quaint little village.

You can't find a lot of quaint in this country anymore. We look like we've been designed by the Mad Architect.

There are hotels with revolving roofs, office buildings that look like they're about to take off for Mars, and 8 zillion sets of golden arches lighting up the midnight sky where quaint used to be.

I visited Helen once, and the word I used to describe it at the time wasn't quaint.

It was "tacky."

But I've changed my mind. "Tacky" is compromising yourself to accommodate an intruder.

"Quaint" is a little guy telling a big guy if he won't play by the rules, he can go jump in the deep fryer.

Hooray for Helen.

4 ELSEWHERE

I've been to several foreign countries
and to just about all over the
Mississippi, one of my favorite places.
Of misplaced symbols of hate and
religious freedom ...

The City of Churches—in the Soviet Union!

Believe it or not, there is a Baptist church in Vilnius, Lithuania.

Or at least there was in 1985.

A member of the group with which I was traveling in the Soviet Union had found out about the church, and maybe twenty of us took cabs to a Sunday service.

The idea of going to a Baptist church in a place controlled by the Soviet Union intrigued us all. Maybe we also thought there was some danger involved.

The church was a small frame building. When we walked in, the service hadn't begun. The congregation was mostly elderly women with their hair hidden under scarves.

Three ministers sat in chairs behind the pulpit. A choir, which numbered about thirty, not including the babies sleeping in some of the choir members' laps, sat behind the ministers in the pulpit.

We were an immediate curiosity. The old women turned their wrinkled faces and tired eyes at us as we stood in the back of the church.

It was like walking into—I would think later—some sort of secret lodge meeting.

An elderly, stooped woman who was seated near where I was standing arose from her chair and motioned for me to take it.

My mother didn't raise me that way. I gestured for her to sit back down. She insisted I sit. A friend said, "She's trying to say it's an honor for us to be in her church. Sit."

So I sat. All three ministers spoke, maybe twenty minutes each. None of us had any idea what any of them were saying, of course, but when the choir sang, it was back home in Pleasant Grove Baptist Church in Heard County, Georgia.

I could recognize, of course, the melody of "Rock of Ages," and then the choir did "The Old Rugged Cross." I was astounded.

After the service, we walked outside the church, and a young man who spoke English came up and said, "We are very happy to have you worship with us. You are Americans, yes?"

We told him we were. We asked him, "Does the government ever try to stop your services?"

He said, "There are so few of us. They mostly ignore us."

Vilnius, the capital of Lithuania, which was taken over by the Soviet Union in 1939, is, literally, the city of churches.

But when the Soviets came in, they turned most of the churches, many of which are magnificent structures, into schools, offices, and museums.

One former church was even transformed into the "Museum of Atheism."

I walked through it. The museum traced religion back to its earliest roots, and the message plainly was that religion is a farce, appealing only to the weak and ignorant.

So I read now that Lithuania has voted to secede from the Soviet Union. If the bold move is successful, I wonder if the little Baptist church—if it still exists—might be able to move into one of the big churches. Let's say the Soviets' Museum of Atheism.

I sort of think "The Old Rugged Cross," in any language, would bounce off those walls and fill the place, so dark and depressing when I was there, with the joyous voices of people free to worship in whatever fashion they choose.

Sing it, brother. Sing it, sister. And, afterward, we'll have dinner on the ground.

Big Brother Is Making Snap Judgments

There always seems to be something new in California that many of us in the rest of the country don't want to see spread eastward. That is because new things in California always seem to be a little scary.

Nobody ate raw fish in the rest of the country until they started doing it in California, did they?

Now, there's Photocop. Not the sequel to the movie *Robocop*, about a giant Polaroid camera with enough firepower to blow away two Iraqs, but a new device to catch more speeders.

You're speeding and you drive past Photocop. It records your speed, takes a picture of your license plate, and also takes a picture of you.

Photocop is such a good camera, according to a California newspaper I read, it can even photograph the expression on your face.

There are a lot of things I don't like about Photocop. I don't like the way it tickets speeders. It doesn't dispatch a live officer to pull you over.

Instead, within twenty-four hours after you've been pinched by

Photocop, its photographs have been processed, you have been identified, and a computer has mailed you a ticket to your home.

That doesn't seem fair. I liked it the old way where cops parked under overpasses or just over the top of a hill or behind those signs you used to see all over the South that said, SAVE AMERICA! IMPEACH EARL WARREN

At least in those instances you had a fighting chance to hit your brakes and sneak past unticketed.

Several California cities say Photocop has greatly enhanced the revenue they make by catching more speeders.

The company that produces Photocop, Traffic Compliance Systems, can say the same thing. Every time Photocop hands out a ticket to a speeder, it pockets fifteen dollars of its own.

Some other thoughts: If Photocop can record the expression on your face, can't it also record the expression on the face of a twenty-two-year-old bimbette you just picked up? Couldn't that lead to blackmail on the part of unscrupulous police officers?

And if Photocop comes south, it could bring an end to a grand Southern tradition, that of the big-bellied county sheriff pulling over the Northern tourist for speeding.

You've seen it enacted on television many times.

The deputy hitches up his pants, walks over to the driver, and says those magical words: "Whar's the far?"

Then he says, "Lemme see yo' dribbinlicunce."

Dribbinlicunce—the little card you carry in your wallet that says the governor of your state has given you permission to operate a motor vehicle.

With Photocop, none of that would be necessary. The Northern speeder will not be pulled over. He'll simply receive a ticket in the mail when he returns to Akron after visiting Crazy Joe's Reptile Farm and Discount Fireworks in Big Snake Beach, Florida.

There's too much Big Brother in Photocop. It's too Orwellian, and what if I'm riding down the road and Photocop nails me and I'm picking my nose?

The right to drive while picking one's nose and not have it

recorded on a photograph back at police headquarters is something every American should stand up and fight for.

If Californians want to give up that freedom, so be it. But don't
bring Photocop east.

Save America. Impeach Photocop.

Frisky Doings at the Mustang Ranch

*Six months from now, Storey County, Nevada, near Reno, at the
famed Mustang Ranch, the legal brothel that filed for bankruptcy
and was turned over to the federal government to run.*

The man has been hot on the craps tables all week, so
he decides he'll splurge a bit at the Mustang Ranch.

He steps into the front door and spots a woman sitting behind
a desk marked "Information."

She is quite attractive, he thinks, if he ignores the fact that she
is popping her gum and has a run in her left black-mesh
stocking—and appears bored.

"Excuse me," he says to the woman, "I came here yesterday,
but you were closed."

"Government holiday," answers the woman. "Somebody's
birthday. Harry Reems, I think."

"But we don't have a holiday for Harry Reems's birthday,"
contests the man.

"We do now, toots," says the woman. "Since Uncle Sam got
into the sex game."

"I see," the man continues, "but two days ago I called, and all
I got was either a busy signal or a recording that said, "Press one

for straight sex; two for kinky; three if perverted, but you must furnish your own chicken.'

"I'm not into chickens, so I pressed two, but nobody ever came on the line."

"Sorry," the woman replies. "That's not my department. So what is it you want?"

"I want to know where the girls are. Don't they come out in their underpants and I get to pick the one I want?"

"Not anymore," says the woman. "First, fill out these forms, and then stand in that line over there to register.

"Then, you come back here and I'll stamp your forms and then you can go stand in that other line to pay the cashier."

"This is ridiculous," says the man. "I just want a girl take to a room."

"You don't pick out a girl anymore. After you see the cashier, you will be assigned a caseworker, and she'll give you an appointment to come back another time. We're currently booking a year from next January."

The man stands in line for two hours and completes all his forms. He meets with a government caseworker, who also appears bored, and gets an appointment for early 1992.

Desperate, he turns back to the woman at the information desk, just back from her break, and pleads, "Look, why can't you and I just go to a room and . . ."

"Are you kidding?" she answers. "That's not my job description. I'm an Administrative Clerk Four. I don't want to jeopardize my retirement."

"That's it for me," says the man. "It's obvious the government is new to this sort of thing."

"Not so fast, sweetcakes," the woman says, "the government has been in this sort of thing, so to speak, for a long, long time.

"Next."

Ole Miss Beaming

OXFORD, MISS.—I lost count of just how many times the University of Mississippi band played "Dixie" last Saturday while the Rebels were upsetting Georgia, 17–13.

The number had to be in the double figures, however.

There were 31,000 at the game. Everybody who wasn't from Georgia had a Confederate flag.

Before the game began, there had been a prayer. And two guys sitting in front of me each brought in a bottle of Jim Beam.

All this prompted my friend Bugar Seely, a veteran Georgia fan, to say, "They still wave the flag, still sing 'Dixie,' they can still pray, and they can still bring liquor into the game. No wonder they beat us."

It hasn't been easy being Mississippi, I was thinking. You read those surveys and Mississippi always seems to come up a loser in such things as education and poverty levels.

And then there was the movie *Mississippi Burning*, which portrayed the entire state as a roost for drawling, ignorant racists.

The University of Mississippi once at least had good football teams to help the self-image. Those were the days of national championships and major bowl games.

But that all went away, too. Ole Miss football has been in a mostly tattered state the last fifteen years.

I guess that's why they celebrated as they did here Saturday when Georgia had fallen.

An Ole Miss football game in Oxford is a trip in a time machine. A trip backward.

Said a Georgia fan, "I was walking through the campus and I saw fraternity boys in coats and ties with their dates, who were in heels. Then, I heard somebody playing 'Dixie' on a trumpet. I kept looking around for Michael J. Fox in *Back to the Future*."

The Georgia band doesn't play "Dixie" anymore. And fear of an American Civil Liberties Union suit has stopped public prayer before Georgia home games.

If you brought a Confederate flag into Sanford Stadium in Athens, Georgia, there'd be a march on the president's office, and security guards check to make certain nobody is bringing any cheering booster into the stadium, too.

After the game here Saturday, students and alumni gathered in a shady lane called the Grove. Ten or so members of the band joined them.

And the Ole Miss people were still waving those flags, and the little band was still playing "Dixie." It was 1958.

So I asked a guy, "How can you people get away with playing 'Dixie,' waving your flags, praying before the game, and bringing booze in?"

"We're not supposed to," he replied. "But we do it anyway."

And where do black people fit into all of this?

The football team was filled with blacks, two members of the miniband were black, and there was a black family standing outside their van, eating chicken and taking an active part in the postgame celebration.

I'm no sociologist, but does it say anything that everybody in that scenario seemed to be getting along nicely?

Maybe Mississippians, both black and white, have it figured out. The key to any sort of co-existence is tolerance, even of symbols that once stood for hate.

Good luck, Rebels, for the rest of the season.

My Motto:
Go East,
Young Man

If I lived in California, I think I would move. It's not that I don't like California. It's one of my favorite states.

San Diego has great weather and a great zoo. Los Angeles has Tommy Lasorda. I've been to Bakersfield a couple of times. Nice people there.

And northern California has wonderful scenery. Name me a city more beautiful than San Francisco.

Venice? I've been there, too, and the water smells like garbage. Paris? No bay.

But if I lived in California, I'd still move.

They've had the Pretty Big One now—the earthquake that measured 6.9 on the earthquake scale that did $7 billion in damage to the San Francisco area. And, of course, the Big One is still to come. I heard a man on television say it could be up to thirty times as powerful as the earthquake that struck just before game three of the World Series.

And what's after that? The Even Bigger One? Could the entire state of California fall into the ocean one day, and suddenly Carson City is the West Coast?

"Life is getting back to normal in San Francisco after the earthquake," a television reporter was saying.

How could life ever be normal there again? How could you ever completely put out of your mind the fact you are living where the earth occasionally shakes the daylights out of everything that is attached to it?

The Pretty Big One. Then, the Really Big One.

For me, living in such a circumstance would be like waiting for the other shoe to drop.

The paper quoted a guy in San Francisco, who said, "I'll never leave here. Where would I go? New York, where muggers hit you on the head and you have to breathe soot?"

That's fine for that guy. Me, I'd quit my job, sell my house, and head East. Even if I couldn't sell my house, I'd head East anyway.

I know I wouldn't be able to sleep anymore if I remained in California. I know I would become neurotic, freeze with fear at any unfamiliar sound, and each time I drove across a bridge, I'd wonder if I were going to make it across without being tossed into the water by an earthquake.

I have friends in San Jose. The day after the earthquake I talked to one of them.

"We didn't get that much damage," she said to me by phone. "But it really frightened the kids."

If I lived in California and had children, that would be another reason I'd move away.

How many nightmares did the earthquake spawn in children? And how long will those nightmares last?

Some adults can deal with living on a ledge. But I'm not certain how many kids can.

There's no question that because I don't live in California, don't have a family there, don't earn my living there, it's fairly easy for me to say I'd get out before another earthquake had a shot at me.

But I wouldn't build a house next door to the ocean, either. Who knows when Hugo's big brother might come back.

And I wouldn't live in New York. Muggers. Soot to breathe. Having no change to tip the doorman.

I think if I were living in California, I'd move to where I live now, Atlanta. We were burned down once, and the Braves and the Falcons are both embarrassments.

But we don't have earthquakes, the air is okay, the muggers mostly mug each other, and about the only thing we have to worry about is whether or not they'll ever finish renovating our freeway system, which they won't. The original plans have been lost.

And most nights in Atlanta, I sleep good. That's something, after California's experience, for which I am thankful.

Room with a . . . Memory

DAYTONA BEACH, FLA.—I had business here. They gave me a room on the top floor of the new Marriott Hotel, which sits on what Daytona always has claimed is "The World's Most Famous Beach."

I looked out the window and, jutting out into the sea, as it has for who knows how many years, was the old dance pier. I would have thought a new hotel or a restaurant that serves salads with odd names and raw fish would have taken its place by now.

Daytona was paradise in my teen years. We came here by the droves on spring break or to celebrate such momentous occasions as finally getting out from under the principal's nose.

I was here in 1963. Me and Clay and Dickey and Charles. We drove my mother's '58 Pontiac to town, and we stayed, the four of us sharing a single room, in a motel named the Palms, or the Blue Shell, or maybe it was Sea Breeze.

Motels at the beach used to have names like that. Then, they were replaced by names like Marriott, Hilton, and Hyatt, not even hotels at all, but *hotels*. Motels are mostly out today, I suppose, gone with the Coppertone Girl and Blatz beer for ninety-nine cents a six-pack.

June of '63. Charles and I found the dance pier. The music

was loud and, Lord, the girls in the short shorts. What was the dance back then? The Twist? The Pony? The Monkey?

I don't remember motel names, and dance crazes fade. But not girls in short shorts.

So we hit on two.

"Where y'all from?" I asked, using my cleverest opening line.

"We're from here," said one of the girls.

Daytona girls. Local girls. What luck.

Local girls, we reasoned, had to be at least a step faster than the visiting sunburned beauties from South Georgia or Michigan. We couldn't understand girls from Michigan, anyway.

I did the talking.

"Look," I said. "We've got some beer back at our motel room. Why don't we go there?"

Lewis, you rascal.

"Sure," said one of the girls, "but we need to get something to eat first."

We took the girls to the first Steak 'n' Shake restaurant I ever saw.

When was the last time these two girls ate? I kept asking that question through the cheeseburgers, the french fries, and the chocolate milkshakes, with extra whipped cream and two cherries, about three bucks' worth for each girl. This was 1963, when three bucks could nearly fill your gas tank.

When the girls finished eating, I said, rakishly, "Y'all ready to go to the motel now?"

One of the girls said, "We have to go to the bathroom first."

That was twenty-seven years ago. We still haven't seen the two Daytona girls again.

I did learn a valuable lesson that night, however. I learned not everybody you buy a cheeseburger for is going to go back to your motel room with you.

I wondered if the old dance pier was still teaching young men such truths like that in the nineties.

I hope so. Cheeseburgers are a lot more expensive now than they were in 1963.

Eyes of Texan's Friends Are Upon Him

There's something I've noticed about Texans who move away from their home state. They never lose their allegiance to their roots.

Tommy (Goose) McDonnell, a friend of mine, is like that.

He was born in Texas. He got into the golf business as a club professional and wound up in Atlanta.

But Tommy had another interest besides golf.

"I'd been wanting to have my own little barbecue joint for years," he told me once.

So he got out of golf and found a run-down building in one of Atlanta's fashionable neighborhoods, renovated it, and opened Texas State Line Barbecue. He raised the Texas flag on the roof of the place he always referred to as "my little barbecue joint."

Texans and Southerners often argue about barbecue. Barbecue to Texans is beef. Barbecue to Southerners is pork.

Tommy had the good sense to serve it both ways. What I liked most about Texas State Line was the ribs, both beef and pork, the cold Lone Star longnecks, and Tommy's jukebox that had Ernest Tubb's immortal "Waltz Across Texas" on it.

Tommy had a rule at Texas State Line. You couldn't wear a tie after six o'clock in the evening. If you did, Tommy would sneak up behind you with a pair of scissors and cut your tie in half.

He even did that to former mayor Andy Young once. He did it to another customer who threatened to sue him.

"I just laughed at him," said Tommy. "I don't want nobody without a sense of humor in my little barbecue joint anyway."

From the first day he opened, Texas State Line brought them in by the droves. That was the reason that when Tommy's lease ran out, the owner of the building wanted to triple the price for renewal.

Tommy told the guy to stuff it up his snout and moved out. And opened up a new place a mile or so away, Texas Line Shack Barbecue.

(I mean to ask Tommy soon what a line shack is. I've been wondering for years because Pat Brady was always saying to Roy Rogers, "Roy, they've got Dale out at the line shack.)

Tommy continued to sell great barbecue at Line Shack, but a new problem arose.

Something happened to his flagpole, and he couldn't raise his Texas flag on the roof. To Tommy, this was a serious problem.

He tried to find somebody to come over and repair the flagpole, but where do you find a flagpole repairman?

Tommy finally decided to try to do the job himself. He got a ladder and climbed onto the roof of Texas Line Shack Barbecue.

He slipped, fell off the roof, and landed on his head in the parking lot. His injuries were severe.

He had to undergo emergency brain surgery to remove a blood clot. He nearly died.

But ol' ex-Texans don't go quietly. He's still in the hospital where he continues to undergo further treatment and rehabilitation.

Tommy McDonnell is one of those rare individuals who would rather do for you than for himself.

The eyes of your friends are upon you, Goose. Get well and get out of there.

We'll have the Lone Star flag flying when you return, if I have to climb up there and do it myself.

I've been to Texas.

5 PET PEEVES

My favorite dog story:

A guy walks up to another guy standing next to a dog. He asks, "Does your dog bite?"

The other guy says, "No."

So the first guy reaches down to pat the dog. The dog bites off two of his fingers.

He says, "I thought you said your dog didn't bite."

And the second guy replies, "That ain't my dog."

A Pet Peeve

There is a lot of discussion concerning animal rights these days. Okay, so what's the deal about the so-called mercy killings of animals?

You know the story. After Ol' Paint stumbles one day, his owner says, "Well, Ol' Paint stumbled, so I guess he's gettin' old. I'll just take out my gun and put a bullet through his head and put him out of his misery."

Unfortunately for Ol' Paint, he's a horse and can't argue his own case by saying, "Hey, put that gun away. I just tripped over a beer bottle."

I hear deer hunters say, "We're doing the deer a favor by killing them."

Overpopulation and that sort of thing. But if I'm a deer, I don't want anybody doing me a favor by blowing my head off with a high-powered rifle.

I admit I am sensitive to this issue because of a personal experience involving the late Plato, a wonderful basset hound I owned in college.

Basset hounds make marvelous pets as long as you can put up with the fact they howl, their ears fall into their food while they eat, and it's impossible to get one out of your favorite chair once it has decided that's where it wants to sleep.

I had owned Plato about a year, and my young bride and I had become quite attached to him.

We had to mop the food that fell off his ears a lot, and when he took up residence in my black Naugahyde reclining chair, I gave in and sat on the couch.

He was that good a dog.

But one day Plato quit eating, a startling occurrence when you consider he once ate a pair of my wife's panty hose.

Plato became listless and started losing weight.

I took him to the vet, who diagnosed a kidney problem. "He's not going to get any better," said the vet. "You might as well put him to sleep"—veterinarian for, "Let me kill your dog."

I told my wife what the vet had said.

"Give me twenty-four hours," she said.

My wife fried three chicken breasts. Plato loved fried chicken before he stopped eating.

She sat up all night with him at the vet's office and tried to feed him small pieces of white meat she pulled from the chicken breast.

About four that morning, she said, Plato finally took a bite, and by eight had eaten all the chicken. He lived to be fourteen.

Now, what inspired all this?

I read a story in the papers the other day that absolutely shocked me.

A woman in Eugene, Oregon, Mary Ann Snoddy, noticed her son's hamster was curled up in the corner of his cage. Because the hamster, Bud, was four, and most hamsters live only a couple of years, she took it upon herself to decide Bud was dying of old age.

She called her vet, who told her to put Bud out of his alleged misery by sticking him in the freezer compartment of her refrigerator overnight. She wrapped poor Bud in a paper sack and put him in the freezer to die.

The next morning, she opened the freezer door to find Bud

had chewed his way out of the sack and had dined on frozen bread and hash browns and was very much alive.

"He sat up on his hind legs," said Mary Ann Snoddy, "as if to say, 'Why did you do this to me?' "

Why, indeed. Putting a hamster in a freezer to do it a favor may be the Snoddyest thing I ever heard of.

If only defenseless animals could file suit.

Oh, Deer, the Hunt Is On

Deer hunting season began Saturday. According to an article I read, there'll be more guys with guns in the woods in my environs just Saturday than there are American troops in Saudi Arabia.

I'll sleep well tonight knowing I'm not only safe from Saddam Hussein, but from the ferocious deer as well.

There was some other deer news in the papers. A jury in Maine brought back an Innocent verdict against a deer hunter charged with manslaughter.

He's out in the woods of Maine and he sees something white, so he takes a couple of shots.

What he saw was a young mother of infant twins, who was in her backyard wearing white mittens. She died from the gunshots.

In her backyard!

A portion of the hunter's defense, I read, was that the dead woman wasn't a native of Maine and didn't know about all the hunting that went on and should not have been in her backyard wearing white mittens.

I'm really not against deer hunting, per se, but I've said all along it could be a much fairer sport (if killing anything can be called a sport) if they would just change some of the rules of the game.

So I have put some great thought into this, and can now offer you Grizzard's Revised Rules of Hunting Down Deer and Blowing Them Away:

- Rule No. 1: If you kill a deer, you have to eat it. None of this trophy killing or shooting a deer for the sheer thrill of seeing it fall.

  We kill cows so that we can have hamburger, so killing a deer in order to have something good to eat, I think, is okay.

  An addendum to Rule No. 1 is you have to eat the entire deer if you kill it. Okay, you don't have to eat the pancreas or the large intestines, but whatever's edible, you've got to eat it all.

  Addendum No. 2 to Rule No. 1 is you can't kill a second deer until you've eaten all your first one.

  If you kill a second deer, a game warden will be sent to your house to check out your freezer and make certain there was none of the first deer left.

  If you kill a second deer before you eat all the first one, you have to eat the pancreas of the second one, but you can prepare it any way you wish. I am a fair man.

- Rule No. 2: You have to hunt in the nude. The deer aren't dressed, are they? All that camouflage is nothing but trickery, and should not be allowed if this thing is to be truly fair. I realize you might get a little nippy out there, and there's all those briars and barbed-wire fences, but, hey, this ain't no Easter egg hunt.

- Rule No. 3: Forget Uzis and bazookas. You can have only one bullet when you go hunting.

  Barney had only one bullet and Andy didn't even carry a gun, and they kept Mayberry safe. Sorry, pal, you missed.

  Go home and get another bullet and you can try tomorrow.

- Rule No. 4: If you do happen to shoot another person by

mistake, it would be quite tacky to ask the family of the departed to allow you to have the head of the victim to put on the wall in the den. Except in Maine, where it's sort of expected.

- Rule No. 5: You cannot at any time say you hunt deer because you (1) are doing the deer a favor by killing them because if you don't, there'll be too many deer and a lot of them will starve; or (2) it's your way of communing with nature.

  If you're worried about the deer starving, why not take some food into the woods and feed the poor things instead of killing them?

  And if all you want to do is commune with nature, get a pair of binoculars and go watch birds. That way if you spot a redheaded, three-toed, black-billed ratbird, there are no rules you have to eat the darn thing, as there are in deer hunting.

- Rule No. 6: If you do not follow Rules 1 through 5, the next time you're in the woods, may Smokey the Bear eat you for your hat, which is what he's been doing to Boy Scouts for years.

The Double Eagle Versus the Armadillo

I'm an animal rights activist. I'm against fur coats, and I'm even against doing anything bad to cats, and I don't like cats.

The reason I don't like cats is they are conniving and arrogant. Cats will sneak behind you and jump on your head, and if you call a cat, the cat will look at you as if to say, "You want me to come over there? Why don't you come over here?"

I don't think we should kill animals, unless they are about to kill us. Not even snakes. People in cars see a snake on the road and they always attempt to run over it.

Why? If you're in a car and you see a snake on the road, the chances of a snake getting inside your car and biting you are pretty slim. I think people run over snakes just for the fun of it, and we animal rights activists say that is wrong.

I bring all this up as background before relating a recent experience.

I was playing golf in Orlando at the lovely Lake Nona course. What makes Lake Nona so delightful is it's away from all urban blight despite the fact it's only ten minutes from the Orlando airport.

There are pristine, natural lakes and deep woods that are alive with many creatures. I've seen deer, a fox, and many armadillos. In fact, armadillos have become a big problem at Lake Nona.

Armadillos, known to many as possums on the half-shell, dig armadillo holes. The armadillo's defense mechanism, as a matter of fact, is to dig a hole and get into it whenever there is danger.

The problem with the armadillos at Lake Nona is they are digging holes all over the golf course, even on the greens.

So, when a friend and I drove up to the 18th tee in our cart and we saw an armadillo rooting around in the grass in the tee box, he said, "The armadillos are ruining the golf course. After we tee off, I'm gonna kill that one."

His tee shot went right. Mine went left. We got back into the golf cart and drove toward the armadillo.

"Let me out of the cart," I said. "I won't be a party to the killing of an animal."

But I did watch. My friend drove over toward the armadillo and pulled out a nine iron from his golf bag. The armadillo, sensing danger, didn't dig a hole and get into it, however.

What the armadillo did was run toward the safety of the woods.

My friend took out after the armadillo with his nine iron. He swung it at the armadillo. He whiffed the armadillo.

He took several more swings at it as he chased the armadillo in hot pursuit. He never did make contact, however, and the armadillo got clean away.

I was greatly relieved.

The way I figure it is that the armadillos were at Lake Nona long before the golfers came.

I assessed my friend a two-stroke penalty, by the way. As the Rules of Golf clearly state: "A player swinging at and missing something as big as an armadillo should be ashamed. Not only from a humanitarian viewpoint but also because an armadillo is about thirty times larger than a golf ball. The guilty player shall be assessed a two-stroke penalty."

As a result of that, I won the match and collected a substantial sum of money.

God bless all the animals, big and small.

Letting the Cat Out of the Bag

They nailed a guy the other day for torturing and killing cats. Seventy-seven of them.

An unemployed law-school graduate, he got five years in jail and ten years on probation.

This individual, according to news reports I read, did some strange things to his victims. He hung some of the cats. He drowned some of them. He chopped up others.

Asked where he got his cats, he answered "free kitten" ads in newspapers.

Reading about all this made me feel sorry for cats for the first time in my life, and played on my conscience to the point that I decided to admit I once did something cruel to a cat myself.

As my mother told the story, when I was three, I brought a stray cat home and put it in our refrigerator. I'm not certain why.

But lucky for the cat, my mother found it before it had an opportunity to freeze or suffocate, whatever it is that might happen to a cat if you put it in a refrigerator.

My mother did have to throw out the bowl of potato salad that was in the refrigerator with the cat, however. Nothing worse than cat hairs in your potato salad.

It is difficult to be indifferent about cats. People who love them usually own three or four and give them the run of their homes.

You go to visit somebody who has cats and eat with them, you can just about expect to have cat hairs in your potato salad, not to mention having cat hairs all over your clothes from sitting on your host's furniture.

People who love cats tie ribbons on them and give them names like Cybil and Roman and probably have become so used to cat hairs in their potato salad they don't even notice it anymore.

People who hate cats, really hate cats. They think cats are sneaky and arrogant.

A cat will sneak up behind you and jump on your head in a heartbeat. That happened to me once when I went to pick up a first-time date in her apartment.

She said, "I'll be just a minute," and disappeared into her bedroom. So I'm sitting there on the couch looking through a copy of *Glamour* I had found on the coffee table that featured a story titled "Are Men Obsolete?" and suddenly my date's cat sneaked up behind me and jumped on my head.

I got kitty off my head and gave it a toss across the room.

"Did you meet, Cybil, my cat?" my date asked me when she finally was ready.

"Do you have anything to treat claw marks on the scalp?" I asked her back.

You call to a dog and a dog will break its neck to get to you. Dogs just want to please. Call to a cat and its attitude is, "What's in it for me?"

Still, I don't think I should ever have put that cat in the refrigerator, and it made me sick to my stomach when I read about the man who tortured and killed seventy-seven cats.

I am glad to see that cat-killer got the slammer. The judge had the option to send him to a psychiatric hospital. She ordered him to receive psychiatric treatment, but she also ordered that it take place behind bars.

I've had a lot of ugly things to say about cats in this space over the years. I don't take any of it back, but I do want cat lovers to know I'm against any harm coming to their pets.

Besides, I've never particularly cared for potato salad, with hair or without, anyway.

6 GOOD ADVICE

There's some stuff about adultery in this chapter, so you might want to turn to it first.

The Write Type

A friend whose son wants to grow up and be a writer asked me what courses the young man should concentrate on in high school.

To answer, I had to look back to my own high school days.

Certainly biology hasn't meant diddley to me as a writer. I could dissect a frog with the best of them in high school, but it hasn't come up since.

Neither has algebra or geometry, and I knew they wouldn't at the time. I basically learned everything I need to know about mathematics in the third grade when they taught me to multiply.

Two times four is eight, which is how many I need to write today so I can take a couple of weeks off and work on my upcoming novel, titled *Don't Get Near Mama, Sailor, She's Been Eatin' Navy Beans.*

Learning about ancient history hasn't benefited me. Who cares when Rome was sacked? It should have had a better offensive line.

And geography. There's a lot of sand in Saudi Arabia. I could have learned that later in life simply by watching U.S. Marines wishing for a cold beer as they wait for President Bush to decide whether or not he's going to get some of them killed.

History. When I was interviewed for this job, nobody asked me anything about Rutherford B. Hayes.

They did teach me grammar and punctuation, but that's why we have editors.

What I finally decided was the most important course I took in sixteen years of schooling was typing.

I have used this skill practically every day of my professional life.

Mr. Sheets, the basketball coach, taught me typing my junior year of high school. Typing teachers usually don't get a lot of credit for molding our youth, but in my case I am certainly beholden to Mr. Sheets.

I'm not certain how many words I now have to my credit, but I type each of them. If you can't type, you're going to be in a helluva mess if you want to be a writer.

In the first place you can't get a job with a newspaper if you can't type. They're going to sit you down at a computer and ask you to produce, and I don't care how much you know about computers, if you can't negotiate the keyboard, nothing readable is going to appear on the screen in front of you.

Some authors, I am told, write out their books in longhand. That's because they never learned to type. If they had, they wouldn't be scribbling on a sheet of paper for months at a time, which can cause severe pain in the hands and fingers.

That's why Edgar Allan Poe wrote all that weird stuff. His hands and fingers were always hurting him. The pain became so intense he began to see talking ravens.

So I told my friend to tell his son to enroll in a typing class as soon as possible.

"But what about foreign languages?" he asked.

"Maybe he ought to learn a little Japanese," I said.

Our golf courses today. Our publishing industry tomorrow. It could happen.

In the Line's Den

A thirty-three-year-old female legal assistant was recently acquitted by jurors in Houston for entering a men's rest room during a concert, which is illegal in Texas. George Strait had been onstage.

I was at a Willie Nelson concert in Atlanta a couple of years ago when a convoy of ladies (more than two) stormed into a men's room where I happened to be standing at the time.

"We just can't wait, boys," said the spokesintruders.

Does this happen at concerts involving noncountry singers? I suppose it has, but it likely happens more at country concerts because (1) there's more beer drinking going on; (2) country-music fans tend to be a little more down-to-earth; and (3) unlike rap concerts, you're not afraid you'll miss the dirty parts while you go to the bathroom.

The woman in Houston, Denise Wells, said, you guessed it, the reason she went into the men's rest room was the line to the ladies' was just too long.

I certainly can sympathize with a woman going into the men's room when nature's call has reached the critical stage.

The desire for relief will cause members of both sexes to do something they might not do otherwise.

Women sportswriters going into men's locker rooms is a professional matter. A woman going into a men's room because she just can't wait has to do with the basic human urge to stop pain.

Men get in and get out of their rest room. Tarry too long and somebody in the back of the line will embarrass you by screaming, "Hey, buddy. You gonna [go] all day?"

But women must look at who's really to blame when they have to resort to going into a men's toilet facility.

They must blame themselves. If women would go into their own rest rooms cognizant of the fact their sisters are waiting on them, this problem could be solved quite easily.

The question of why women take so long in the bathroom has always intrigued me. I even wrote a country song about the issue, titled "When My Love Returns From the Ladies Room, Will I Be Too Old to Care?"

After the song followed a book of the same name, and Hollywood will be out with the movie as soon as enough extras can be located for the long-line-to-the-ladies-rest-room scene.

To put an end to this problem and keep the issue out of our courts, women need to pick it up a bit. Try these ideas:

1. Keep your undergarments to a minimum when you go to a concert.
2. Don't wear anything with a lot of snaps, zippers—or a key. Why not give Velcro a chance?
3. Comb your hair and powder your nose somewhere else. There are people in line turning blue.
4. If somebody asks you, "Where did you get those darling earrings?," wait until you both get outside to answer.

For further instructions, you might want to pick up my soon-to-be-published sequel to *When My Love . . .* etc., titled *Is It Time for a Shot Clock in Women's Rest Rooms?*

Why Not Walk Away from the Oil Crisis?

We could walk a lot more in this country. That's what I said. We could actually walk more.

If we walk more and drive our cars less, then maybe we could become less dependent on foreign oil so when some sheikh of the burning sands decided to take over Lower Oilrichabia, we could ignore him.

There wouldn't be any need to send over our troops and planes, no reason to worry about chemical warfare, no reason to bug Henry Kissinger for interviews, no reason to bring up that nasty word "Armageddon," no reason to have to pay $87.50 a gallon at the neighborhood Texaco, and no reason for Dan Quayle to say, "Please, George, don't die on me now."

I used to walk all the time. Before I got a bicycle, I had to walk practically everywhere I couldn't convince an adult to drive me.

If I got thirsty and my mother said, "Walk, it'll be good for you," when I asked her to drive me to a store for a big orange, I'd have to hoof it a half-mile to the store and back.

I even walked all the way to Bobby Entrekin's house one day. It was two miles both ways. He had invited me over to play cowboys and punk rockers.

But it was a pleasant, enlightening experience.

On the way, I saw a dead opossum in the road, I found a pointed rock that could have been an arrowhead, I kicked an empty can at least a mile, and I had a lot of time to think about what I wanted to do when I grew up.

I decided the next time an adult asked me about it, I would

say, "I want to star in porno films," and see the look that would bring.

But after I got my bike and then got old enough to drive, I gave up walking, as have many of us.

Two of the three times I got married, I drove down the aisle. The other time, I took a cab.

I probably would drive between rooms in my house, but my car won't fit through the front door.

We are slaves to our automobiles and the juice that makes them run and that gets us into harm's way and allows oil companies to make us all feel like a bunch of dipsticks for what we have to pay for gasoline.

Let's all start walking more and driving less. We could start with me.

The convenience store where I buy pork and beans and copies of the *Enquirer* is less than a half-mile away. I could walk there.

I could walk to the Waffle House for my weekly cholesterol IV.

I could walk to the video store to rent *Naughty Female Attorneys* and *Debbie Does Fargo, North Dakota*, neither of which I had a part in, incidentally.

I could walk to a friend's house to play cowboys and rap groups, and I could walk to my ex-girlfriend's house when I forget I am an insensitive, arrogant, selfish jerk and need to be reminded.

Join me, America. Let's go for a walk and give Ahab the Arab and John D. Rockerperson a bad case of gas.

Keeping Your Cool in the Good Old Simmer Time

Dr. Grizzard's Several Ways to Beat the Heat:

- Don't Go Outside: This is the most common mistake people make when there is a heat wave. They go outside. That's where it's hot, you ninny.

   Inside, there's air-conditioning and ice and shade. Outside, you can't breathe and you'll sweat and start to smell bad.

   But you say, "I have to go outside in order to get to work."

   That's another thing. Avoid work. The only things that work in hot weather are mules and fools. Call in hot.
- Don't Wear Any Underwear: This will enable you to avoid one of the really unpleasant circumstances that can occur during a heat wave.

   You can get what is commonly known as boxer bundle. The hotter it gets, the more your boxers will want to ride up. And before you know it, your boxers will be in a tiny wad and might even have to be removed surgically.
- Avoid Hot Weather Clichés: This won't make you any cooler temperature-wise, but it will make you cooler as in, "That guy's really cool. Look at his six-hundred-fifty-dollar sneakers."

   Some examples of hot weather clichés to avoid:

1. "Hot enough for you?"
2. "It's not the heat, it's the humidity."

3. "Gonna be a scorcher today."
4. "Hot, ain't it?"
5. "One of these days, I'm gonna own this construction company. Hand me another drink of that ice water, Harvey."

• Cool Thing to Say If Somebody Asks You to Play Tennis at Lunchtime: "Are you nuts? Only mad dogs and Englishmen go out in the noonday sun."
• Drink Lots of Liquids: Which is redundant. The only thing you can drink is liquids, so just drink.

But avoid prune juice and buttermilk, and if your hand turns blue, don't be alarmed. It's just the result of its being in the beer cooler all afternoon. The color will return before Thanksgiving.

• Do Not Watch Television Weather Forecasts: They will only make you more uncomfortable by saying things like: "Well, for the rest of the week there's no relief in sight. It's going to be hot, hazy, and humid."

Didn't we already know that? It's July. It's supposed to be hot, hazy and humid. We don't need to be reminded.

Television weather forecasts would be better if they told us things we didn't know, like why some idiots continue to jog in this kind of weather, how long you can remain in a cold shower before you begin to wrinkle and shrink, and, speaking of relative humidity, how much you perspire while having sex with your cousin.

• Don't Get into Arguments, That Will Only Make You Hotter: If somebody says something that is totally incorrect or offensive, let it go until December.

Then, look them up and say, "Look, you ignorant airhead, Miami is NOT the capital of Florida and my wife does NOT have thick, hairy ankles."

If they want to press either issue, it's okay to resort to violence. Even dingbats who jog in July know Tallahassee is the capital of Florida and your wife's ankles aren't that thick and hairy for a woman who goes 280 and wears a mustache.

• Take Up an Indoor Hot-Weather Hobby: It will take your mind off the heat.

Strip checkers can be fun. So is seeing how long you can hold two ice cubes under your armpits before they melt, whether or not you can make yourself fit into the freezer section of your refrigerator, and listening to your Willie Nelson Christmas album, especially "Frosty the Snowman," "Jingle Bells," and, a personal favorite of mine, "Santa, If You Want to Keep the Beer Real Cold, Put It Next to My Ex-Wife's Heart."

Dr. Grizzard must go now. It's his move.

Adult Tale of Adultery

The story I am about to tell has to do with adultery. Let me say, however, that by telling this story, I am in no way condoning adultery.

Adultery is one of the major-league thou-shalt-nots, and adultery can be the cause of major-league pain.

But it does happen, and one of the things that is always on the mind of a person who cheats on his or her spouse is, "What would I do if I got caught?" There are several theories of how to handle such a frightening experience.

One says never to admit anything, no matter how much evidence there is against you—the old it's-my-story-and-I'm-sticking-to-it routine.

Another idea is to put the blame on the accuser.

Say, "I wouldn't have the need to go to somebody else if you didn't come to bed every night with your hair in curlers."

Or, in a case where the wife is the cheater, "I wouldn't have the need to go to somebody else if you would bathe more often."

I thought I had heard all the ways to deal with being caught until I heard the following story.

The two individuals who told it swear it is true, and I have no reason to doubt them.

Here it goes: This man lived with his wife in one town but had a branch office, for which he was responsible, in another town, a four-hour drive from his home.

Four or five times a month, he would go to the other town on business, and on one of his trips, he became involved with another woman. After that, his trips to the other town became more frequent and lasted longer. His wife became suspicious.

So the man left one day by plane on another of his trips.

The next day, his wife got into her car and drove the four hours to the other town. She did some excellent detective work and came up with the name and address of her husband's lover.

She drove to the apartment and knocked on the door. Her husband answered it. There they stood, face to face.

The man never hesitated. Without speaking a word, he slammed the door behind him, locking it and leaving all his possessions. He ran past his wife, got into his rental car, and drove away.

He went directly to the airport and caught a flight home. He ditched the clothes he was wearing and changed. When his wife returned home hours later, he asked indignantly, "Where in the hell have you been?" She said, "You've been having an affair. I saw you at your lover's apartment."

He said, "Are you crazy? I got back home this morning. How could you have seen me there when I was here?" The man stuck to his story, never wavering. According to the people who passed the tale along to me, the man's wife, probably wanting desperately to believe him, finally accepted his innocence. He never went back to see his lover, and the marriage continued.

If you are currently having an affair, you might want to store this away, because you're eventually going to get caught. All who cheat eventually get caught.

It's God's way of telling you to find another hobby.

7 THE SPORTING LIFE

I used to be a sportswriter. I got out of it, however, when I decided I could not go into another locker room and try to interview a three-hundred-pound naked man.

Why I Get No Kick Out of Soccer

Twenty-one reasons why I hate soccer and wouldn't pay attention to a World Cup match if it was going on in my backyard and the beer was free:

1. There are only three final scores in soccer. They are 0–0, 1–0, and in a real scoring orgy, 1–1.
2. Being able to bounce a ball off one's head isn't that impressive to me. I've seen countless seals do the same thing on *The Ed Sullivan Show*.
3. Soccer breeds fan violence because it's very dull, and when the fans get bored, they pass the time by trying to kill and maim one another.
4. Nobody ever throws a high, inside fastball in soccer, baseball's answer to killing and maiming.
5. A man named Phil Woosnam, then president of the North American Soccer League, once bragged to me, "In twenty years, soccer will be bigger than pro football in the United States." That was twenty-five years ago.
6. Soccer is responsible for soccerstyle kickers in American football. I agree with the late Norman Van Brocklin, who

was asked his reaction to the game, after his Atlanta Falcons had been beaten on a last-minute field goal by some guy from Yugoslavia or Afghanistan.

Van Brocklin said, "They ought to tighten the immigration laws in this country."

7. It was a referee's controversial call in a soccer match that started World War I.

No, I can't prove that, but I don't have to.

8. Too many soccer teams wear dark socks with their shorts, a violation of every fashion law ever written.

9. The theme song for the British Broadcasting Corporation's coverage of the World Cup is Luciano Pavarotti's version of "Nessu Dorma," from Puccini's opera Turandot.

The theme song of WGN's coverage of the Chicago Cubs baseball is Harry Caray singing "Take Me Out to the Ball Game."

10. If soccer were an American politician, it would be Alan Cranston.

11. If it were an American actress, it would be Florence Henderson.

12. Parents of kids who play soccer in American schools are overbearing and obnoxious. It's because they are secretly upset their kids were too wormy to try out for football.

13. My alma mater, the University of Georgia, overcame all sorts of odds and won the College Baseball World Series. I realize that doesn't have a thing to do with soccer, but I just thought I would mention it.

14. If Georgia has a soccer team, I am blissfully unaware of it.

15. Bo doesn't know diddley about soccer.

16. I was in London once and watched the Super Bowl of British soccer matches on television because there wasn't anything else on. The two teams ran up and down the field for approximately three hours, but nobody could score.

They decided to play another game two nights later. I watched that, too. I'd seen all the churches, museums, and china shops I wanted to see by that time.

They ran up and down the field again for an hour or two, and then the ball hit a player in the head and went into the goal completely by accident, and the final score was 1–0. When the game was over, two guys came on the screen and analyzed it for forty-five minutes.

17. If soccer were a vegetable, it would be asparagus.
18. Hitler was probably a soccer fan.
19. Parents of American children who play soccer will react violently to number 12 and write me a lot of nasty, threatening letters. Hey, it's what they deserve for raising wimps.
20. If soccer were an American soft drink, it would be Diet Pepsi.
21. How 'bout them Dawgs.

Ted, It's Time to Apologize to Braves Fans

Ted Turner went around last week apologizing for another couple of stupid things he said recently.

First, he apologized to Chinese students for defending Chinese leaders' butchering of protesters in Tiananmen Square.

Was Hitler just doing his job?

Then, he went to a Baptist church and apologized for saying Christianity is a religion for losers.

So what's Buddhism, a religion for fat people?

Ted Turner has put his foot in his mouth so many times over the years, his front teeth are starting to protrude.

Remember when your mother warned, "Stop sucking your thumb, your teeth are going to protrude"?

Same thing can happen when you routinely have to suck on a Gucci shoe because your brain loses temporary contact with your tongue.

Turner said, "It's apology week."

But I think he forgot somebody. I think he forgot to apologize to fans of the Atlanta Braves, the joke of a major-league baseball team he owns.

I admit it. My name is Lewis (Hi, Lewis), and I'm a Braves fan. What Ted Turner says about Chinese leaders and how he describes Christianity are mind-boggling, but a lot of people have weird opinions, none of which affect me much.

What does affect me, however, is I live in Atlanta and the Atlanta Braves are twenty-five years old and they are still in last place.

Does Ted Turner apologize for that?

It's the same every summer. I get pumped up during spring training, and I think to myself, With a little luck and another good year out of Lonnie Smith, the Braves might have a good season.

What am I, some kind of dreamer? They used to say pulling for the New York Yankees was like pulling for U.S. Steel.

Pulling for the Braves is like pulling for a Democratic nominee for president. It's your classic effort in futility.

What I think Ted Turner should do is let everybody into Atlanta Stadium one night for free, and before the game—to be televised on his national cable network—he should get down on his knees at home plate and apologize for the dogs of summer he has tried to pawn off on Atlanta as a major-league baseball team.

He should apologize for allowing the trade of brilliant prospects Brett Butler and Brook Jacoby to Cleveland for washed-up pitcher Len Barker.

For those who don't follow baseball, it was like trading two T-bone steaks for an onion.

He should apologize for the years of poor hitting and worse

pitching. He should apologize for putting the Braves on TV from Key West to Cold Nose, Alaska. As an Atlantan, I wish we could have kept the Braves our little secret, sort of like having an alcoholic uncle.

The Braves ruin my summer every year. If the Braves were a movie, they would be playing at a drive-in where the speakers don't work.

My main question is, How can a man who owns a baseball team that shames an entire city—and makes TV viewers look forward to the end of its games so that they can watch wrestling—call anybody or anything losers?

Say you're sorry, Ted. A city and a bored national television audience await.

He Won't Let His Career Go Down the Drain

Andre Hastings of Georgia is one of the most talented high school football players in the country.

Get the ball near Andre, he can catch it.

Everybody wants Andre. Notre Dame wants him. Michigan wants him. Georgia and Georgia Tech, of course, want to keep him in the state.

Here's what I like most about Andre:

We've all heard those recruiting stories. Young recruits demand cars, clothes, sex, and money to sign, and, quite often, they get what they ask for.

I even knew of a respected Southern school that was recruiting a young man who wanted to become a doctor.

So, the kid was taken to the hospital on campus, given a robe and allowed to sit in on a hysterectomy.

But none of that for Andre Hastings. What he wants in a school that signs him is simple. He wants his own bathroom.

"I want to have my own separate bathroom," Andre was quoted as saying in the Sunday sports section.

"That's a personal thing with me," he went on. "I just don't want to share a bathroom, and I've told coaches that."

Michigan seems to be in big trouble with Andre. He visited Ann Arbor and said, "I've been led to believe I'd have to share a bathroom with an entire dorm hall there."

I'm thinking of the reaction coaches are having to this unique situation.

"Dammit," says Coach Norman Hardrock of Cheat U., "I've got six BMW convertibles and three cheerleaders to give away, and this kid wants a private bathroom. We got any alumni who are plumbers?"

I don't blame Andre for wanting his own, as the author of the Sunday piece put it so well, "private potty."

When I was in college, I had to share a bathroom with an entire dorm hall. I didn't go to Michigan, but that was the toilet situation at the University of Georgia.

You get nineteen guys in the bathroom at the same time and you've got to wait in line for the shower, and inevitably some bully starts going around attempting to pop a wet towel on your bare backside.

It was worse after I got married and had to share a bathroom with my wife. Women will hang wet panty hose on the shower rod and cover the sink area with an assortment of exotic shampoos and oils, not to mention spare parts for their Volvo station wagons.

At least in college nobody ever took my razor to shave his legs, which often happened to me when I was married.

Of course, if somebody had taken my razor to shave his legs, I would have sought an immediate transfer to another housing unit.

We know not the reason why young Mr. Hastings is suffering from flushophobia, the fear of having to share a bathroom, but it could be from some traumatic experience he underwent as a child, such as being frightened by a can of Drano when he was three.

I'm also not certain if providing a private bathroom for high school recruits is against the rules of the National Collegiate Athletic Association, which governs such things.

But if it's not, after the season my beloved Georgia Dawgs had last year, I'd suggest they start now on the Andre Hastings Private Bathroom Complex.

I'll donate four towels, a couple of bars of soap, and a rubber duckie myself.

Top that, Notre Dame.

Hockey Cuts No Ice with Me

ATLANTA—A friend called Tuesday and invited me to go to a hockey game.

"Where is the game?" I asked him.

There is no hockey team in Atlanta anymore. There used to be a team, the Flames, but it moved to Nova Scotia or Cleveland or Saskatchewan, I can't remember which.

"The game's not in Nova Scotia or Cleveland or Saskatchewan?" I asked my friend. "I don't want to go to any of those places."

"No," he said. "There's a hockey game right here in Atlanta tonight."

He went on and explained that the Boston Bruins and the Philadelphia Flyers were playing an exhibition hockey game at the Omni, and his boss had given him two tickets and told him to go.

I'm not certain what my friend did wrong to deserve such treatment from his boss, but it must have been pretty bad.

I figured the least I could do was go with him and help him get through the ordeal.

I had attended a few hockey games back when Atlanta had its own team. I had heard of hockey, of course, and knew it was popular in places where it got so cold people suffered brain damage and paid to go to hockey games, but that was the extent of my knowledge.

I can report now, nothing much has changed about hockey since I was introduced to it. It's the same old dull stuff that it was years ago.

The players still wear skates and play the game on ice and the ball they use is flat and they call it a "puck," which is a stupid name for a ball, even if it is flat.

The idea is to skate back and forth on the ice for hours attempting to put the puck in an opponent's goal.

That doesn't occur often, however, and most of the game involves the players simply skating back and forth, which is interesting for about eleven seconds.

And when somebody does put a puck into a goal, the puck is so small you never actually see the entry.

That's why somebody turns on a red light when a goal is scored, so everybody will know it's time to either stand up and cheer or feel depressed, depending on which side you're on.

Then, there's fighting. What happens is that when one of the hockey players gets bored skating back and forth, he starts a fight.

But the fighting isn't all that interesting, either, because the players involved put down their sticks and grab one another and do more dancing and hugging than fighting.

If the players would attempt to beat each other over the heads with their sticks, it would improve hockey fighting a great deal—that, or allow them to carry knives.

There were fourteen thousand people at the game. I'm not certain how many of them came on their own accord and how many were being punished by their bosses, as in the case of my friend, but the attendance was high enough that the sports pages speculated next day on whether or not Atlanta might get its own hockey team again.

I hope not. If we had a hockey team again, my boss could get mad at me and assign me the hockey beat, and I'd have to watch hockey games until I became brain-damaged, too.

There's another reason I hope nobody brings hockey back to Atlanta. We've already got Braves baseball and Falcons football. Isn't that enough agony for one city?

Super Bore

The Super Bowl party I went to Sunday began to fall apart soon after the start of the second quarter. That's early even for a Super Bowl party.

According to a study by the University of That Part of Idaho That Looks Like a Stick, most Super Bowl parties last at least into the third quarter before partygoers lose interest in the game and leave the television set to go back into the kitchen and hang out near the bar.

There's been a quarter of a century of Super Bowls, and most of them have had all the drama of the 1980 presidential election when Ronald Reagan was pronounced a winner over Jimmy

Carter before the two candidates even got up to shave on Election Day.

We go through two weeks of hype and anticipation as we await the game that decides the champion of all professional football.

Millions of dollars are bet on the game. Millions of dollars are spent on dip and booze for Super Bowl parties.

And then Super Sunday arrives, and we watch Hitler invade Poland again.

This most recent Super Bowl wasn't even that close. Poland held out for a month against the German blitzkrieg.

Denver barely got off a shot against San Francisco.

It was men against a Girl Scout troop. It was Mike Tyson against Don Knotts. It was Emerson Fittipaldi racing against a three-legged mule.

If Sunday's game had been a chain of department stores, it would have declared bankruptcy and asked protection from its creditors long before halftime.

I had just settled into some shrimp dip with Wheat Thins when the 49ers scored first. Before I could get to the brie, they had scored twice more.

With twelve minutes to go in the half, I lost interest in the game, left the television set, and went to the kitchen and hung out around the bar.

I got into a discussion on foreign affairs with another guy who had forsaken the game, too.

"Did you hear they sentenced Noriega?" he asked me.

"I hadn't heard."

"They came down on him hard," the man explained. "He's got to coach football at the University of Alabama for five years."

Soon, there wasn't anybody at the party paying attention to the Super Bowl, although there were several calls to bookies to get the halftime line on the Bud Bowl, which at least stayed close.

It's time the National Football League did something about the Super Bowl for the millions who are disappointed each year.

First, the NFL should make the 49ers trade some of their

players for some of the Atlanta Falcons players. No matter who the Falcons got, they would still be lousy, as God obviously intended, and at least the 49ers would then have their own share of slow-footed, dim-witted bums like the other teams.

The NFL also could make a rule that if one Super Bowl team got ahead of the other by 21 points, the team leading would have to play without their helmets until the other team caught up.

A few other thoughts would be to allow the underdog team to carry knives, to make Joe Montana throw left-handed, and to allow any team getting severely beaten to leave the field before the end of the game and get back on the bus in order to save themselves further embarrassment.

The rest of the TV time could be spent on mud-wrestling, featuring John Elway as the mud.

Atlanta Brave-ly Faces the New Season

Think, Braves fans, what it would have been like if the lockout had continued and there had been no major-league baseball season in 1990.

The Braves wouldn't have made any stupid errors or dumb trades. They wouldn't have been mathematically eliminated from the pennant race at the end of Opening Day, and it would have been a year to remember.

But, no. The Braves will play in 1990 after all, and here, sadly, is my month-by-month prediction of what to expect:

- April: Shortstop Andres Thomas will balk at the decision to move him to third base and will announce he will hold his breath until he is put back at shortstop. Manager Russ Nixon will leave Thomas at shortstop, and Dale Murphy will be traded to Toronto for a minor-league third baseman who at least has one good eye.

  The Braves will win three games. Ted Turner will acquire Switzerland.

- May: General Manager Bobby Cox will fire manager Nixon and replace him with the late Billy Martin.

  The Braves will win seven games. Their new third baseman, hitting .098, will go on the disabled list with the gout.

- June: The Braves will win four games. Announcer Skip Caray will say he can't take it anymore and will pursue a new career as a lambada dance instructor.

  Ted Turner will trade Switzerland for the rights to begin an all-Gidget cable movie channel in reunified Germany.

- July: First baseman Nick Esasky, who was acquired from the Boston Red Sox in the off-season, and who signed a three-year, $5.6 million contract, will retire and join a religious cult headed by another of his former managers, Pete Rose, who will have changed his name to Shahna Abdullah Ubetcha.

  The late Billy Martin will be fired as manager and will be replaced by the late Casey Stengel. The Braves will win five games, but nobody will notice.

- August: shortstop Andres Thomas will demand to be moved to right field because there's less stress out there. The Braves will trade sensational pitcher John Smoltz to the Dodgers for a rookie shortstop who still wets the bed.

  The Braves, in a spurt, will win eleven games and move within ninety-four games of the division-leading Padres.

- September: Billionaire Donald Trump will acquire the Braves from Ted Turner and announce his new bride, Marla, will dress up like an Indian princess and sing the national anthem before all home games.

Trump will say, "The kid's got talent. You'll see. You'll see."

The Braves won't win any games and will set a new major-league record for the most losses in a single season.

· October: Mercifully, the season will end. Dale Murphy will be named the Most Valuable Player in the American League. John Smoltz will pitch the Dodgers to victory in the World Series.

Donald Trump will acquire NBC and replace Debby Norville with Marla.

The Falcons will lose to Philadelphia, Phoenix, Indianapolis, and Tampa Bay, and head coach Jerry Glanville will be replaced by the late George Halas.

Play ball!

Superhero:
He Fits It to a Tee

If you took a poll, I think you would find most American sports fans wanted an Australian named Greg Norman to win the recent Masters Golf Tournament.

He came close. A bogey on the last hole of the tournament cost him a spot in the sudden-death play-off, eventually won by Nick Faldo.

I don't have anything against Nick Faldo, but he simply isn't the individual we need—a professional golfer to emerge as a superhero.

We really haven't had a golfer we could adore since Arnold Palmer and the glory of the late fifties and early sixties, the years that immediately preceded the destruction of Camelot, the turmoil of the civil rights movement, the agony of Vietnam, Nixon, and the American League's decision to adopt the designated hitter.

Palmer was our kind of guy, a guy who rarely played it safe. He always attacked, even when the smart money said not to.

He was Merriwellian and Ruthian, and he was, of course, the General and his army. General Georgie Patton, if you want a name.

But Palmer's putting eye went, and a fat kid named Jack Nicklaus started winning all the tournaments that Palmer once had.

But we never took to Nicklaus like we did Palmer, and only in the last years of Nicklaus's prime did we accept him and give him his due respect.

But whom do we have now? Lee Trevino thrilled us with two good rounds at Augusta last week, but his was a fairy tale that lasted for only half the tournament.

Gentle Ben Crenshaw is, well, just too gentle to succeed a Palmer. Tom Watson's best is behind him. Tom Kite wears glasses. Mark Calcavecchia lacks the regal style to be a general. Seve Ballesteros has the aura of a pouter. Nick Faldo has proven he can play a lick—but trust me, Nick Faldo ain't it.

It's got to be Greg Norman. He even carries himself on a golf course like Palmer. He charges like the General of old. He is a man who lives for challenge.

I played in a foursome with Norman once. He was an absolute gentleman. A friend was caddying for me, and after Norman had hit his drive on a par 5, my friend said to him, "This is the only par five on the tour that *Golf Digest* says no pro can hit in two."

"Oh, really?" said Norman, asking for a three-wood and flying his ball completely over the green on his subsequent shot. My friend was speechless.

Sports heroes, I still believe, are good for us. They are escapes from otherwise mundane lives. They inspire the youth. They offer relief from news of environmental disasters, schoolyard massacres, and something else that causes cancer.

And golf is where we should look now for this sort of individual.

Basketball and football? Too many guys on dope. Baseball? There seem to be too many major-league players with too much testosterone and too little judgment, and now they're saying Pete Rose made as many bets as base hits.

I can call on my experience as a sportswriter to tell you that of professional athletes I dealt with, golfers were easily the best educated, the best mannered, the best groomed, the most eloquent, and the least likely to spit or scratch in an inappropriate place while appearing on national television.

The rap on Greg Norman is he can't win a major tournament. Well, there are three left in this golfing season: the United States Open, the British Open, and the PGA, and wouldn't it do him, not to mention the rest of us, a lot of good if he'd win just one of them?

C'mon, mate. We need you.

Write Solution to Locker-Room Hassle

There's a simple solution to this thing about women sportswriters in men's locker rooms.

Sportswriters, male and female, should just quit going to locker rooms.

Sportswriters used to watch ball games and then just wrote what happened. They were critics, many of them brilliant.

But then somebody got the idea to go into locker rooms after the games were over and ask coaches and players what they thought happened.

Quote marks started getting in the way of good writing.

Covering a football game isn't exactly like covering a budget crisis. A guy runs with the ball and another guy tries to take his head off. What's to ask?

I was a sportswriter in a previous life. I never heard a good question asked in a locker room except for the time a coach answered an inquiring sportswriter with a question of his own.

That question went, "What are you asking me for? Didn't you see the game?"

Sportswriters are notorious for asking stupid questions in locker rooms.

Once, I asked a Georgia Tech football player who had intercepted a pass and ran it back for a touchdown, "What were you thinking while you were running down the field?"

He answered, "Nothing."

What did I think he was thinking? Whether or not Hitler made a mistake by invading Russia?

Sometimes sportswriters ask other sportswriters dumb questions. My former colleague Frank Hyland, of the *Atlanta Journal*, used to cover the Braves.

He asked the great Henry Aaron a question Aaron didn't like.

Aaron happened to be eating a can of strawberries at the time.

He threw the strawberries into Hyland's face.

Later, I asked Frank, "What did you think when Aaron hit you with the strawberries?"

He answered, "I was thinking, Hey, these are pretty good strawberries."

I hated going into the locker rooms when I was covering sports. They were hot and crowded and smelly, and I could never get used to interviewing large naked men.

I always felt I was invading their privacy, and I could never shake the notion that interviewing large, naked men was a lousy way to make a living.

If I were Lisa Olson of the *Boston Herald*, I'd tell my editor, "Listen, I can write better than those guys (the New England Patriots) can talk. I'll cover the games, and when they are over, I'll write what I saw and what I think about it."

Besides, who wants to read some born-again wide receiver saying, "Well, you know, first of all, you know, I want to thank, you know, my personal Lord and Savior, Jesus, you know, Christ."

I think sportswriting would be a lot better if today's writers had to rely on their own abilities to put words together instead of simply regurgitating the boring quotes of the coaches and athletes they talk to in quarters that are for bathing and dressing, not press conferences.

Lisa Olson has every right to do her job. So let her do it.

Write, Lisa. Be a critic, not a quotetaker. Show us some wit and bite and don't worry about missing any interesting locker-room quotes.

Jockstrap eloquence is a rare thing, indeed.

8 FLIGHTS OF FRIGHT

Ever notice the first thing you see at an
airport? It's a big sign that says, TERMINAL.
Have a nice flight.

Is That Any Way
to Run an Airline?

As everybody who keeps an eye on the commercial-airline game knows, Eastern Airlines is flat broke.

Of course, so is Donald Trump, singer Billy Joel, and the United States of America.

Trump overbuilt, Joel let his brother-in-law handle his finances, and the United States of America is run by politicians, so what did you expect?

There are a lot of reasons Eastern is hanging in the skies by a thread. Frank Lorenzo, whom Eastern employees would like to see hanging by a rope, is one.

But what I wanted to know is how the airline is intending to cut expenses in an effort to remain in the air.

So I contacted an Eastern source, who asked his (or her) name not be used.

Know, however, this person is a key cog in the Eastern chain of command and was willing to talk to me in order that Eastern customers would know the airline is digging in to save itself.

"What are some of the ways you are going to cut back?" I asked my source.

"Magazines," the source replied. "You just don't realize how much an airline has to spend on magazines and other reading material for passengers to peruse while in flight.

"From now on we'll have just one copy of USA *Today* aboard, and passengers will have to pass it around and take turns reading it."

"What else?" I wanted to know.

"We're doing away with seat cushions," was the answer.

"But what about the fact the passengers could use their seat cushions for flotation?"

"That's a bunch of baloney, anyway. Ever see anybody at the beach floating on an airline seat cushion?

"Of course not. Passengers are just told their seat cushions will float so they won't be nervous when we fly over water."

"What are the passengers going to sit on?"

"They'll all be asked to bring their own pillows."

"How about the oxygen masks that are supposed to fall down in the unlikely event of cabin depressurization?"

"They're gone, too," said my source. "Also I'd suggest passengers bring their own oxygen tanks aboard from now on."

"How will the crew be affected?"

"We're cutting out navigators," I was told.

"But isn't that dangerous? How would the pilot know which way to fly?"

"It'll just have to be on instinct. If a flight leaves Philadelphia for Atlanta, for instance, the pilot will know to head south and start slowing down when he sees Stone Mountain."

"How about flight attendants?"

"We won't need any. We're cutting out all drinks and meals. Just can't afford it."

"Cutting out the meals sounds like a great idea to me," I said, "since nobody likes airline food anyway. But how can you do away with drinks?"

"We're strongly suggesting each passenger get sloshed before he or she gets on the plane, and they just might also want to bring a bottle with them for the flight."

"Why is that?"

"We're doing away with our mechanics."

"No mechanics at all?"

"If there's a problem before takeoff, we'll ask for volunteers from the passengers who might know something about repairing an airplane."

"What if nobody volunteers? Are you still going to take off?"

"We'll take a chance. Columbus did."

"Think the public will go for all this?" I asked.

"We'll be offering great discounts," said the person from Eastern. "You can get a round-trip ticket from anywhere we fly for $24.17 if you bring along your own toilet paper."

Phobias at Forty Thousand Feet

It's the law: You can't smoke on a commercial airliner unless you're flying to Tibet.

That's because nonsmokers raised a lot of hell when they heard you could get cancer from secondhand smoke.

So now you thought it was safe to go back to 36E. Not so fast.

I was reading *Time* the other day and saw an article titled "Danger at 40,000 Feet."

It didn't mention anything about secondhand smoke, but it did mention a government study that says you can get zapped by a lot of cosmic radiation from the sun and stars when you fly.

Time said the study indicated that among 100,000 crew members, who flew for twenty years, 600 of them would die premature cancer deaths because of the radiation they would get through the thin skin of their planes.

Passengers are at a risk, too. Especially frequent flyers, such as myself.

That's great. Something new to worry about when I fly, and I fly a lot, and flying scares me for a lot of reasons, such as I don't understand how something larger than a Greyhound bus can get off the ground and stay there.

I barely muddle through when I fly, but stewardesses like me. They lose a lot of weight running back and forth between me and wherever they keep those little bottles of courage.

Fear of flying is a phobia, of course. **Temporary Morgueaphobia:** the fear of winding up under a sheet in a high school gymnasium.

But the problem for those affected is there are all sorts of other little phobias that come under the heading of the primary one.

There is **Glubglubaphobia,** for instance, which is the fear that if you ever, in fact, need to use your seat cushion for flotation, it won't work and you will drown in whatever farm pond or backyard swimming pool your flight has crashed into.

Over the years I have compiled a list of many phobias I fall victim to when I fly. Which of these do you have?

- **Whirraphobia:** fear of any change in engine sound.
- **Iranaphobia:** fear of the airplane being hijacked by Arab terrorists who have a thing for Southern guys with mustaches.
- **Jimmydeanaphobia:** fear that those little sausage patties they serve me on breakfast flights aren't cooked well enough and I will get trichinosis.
- **Notimeforgoodbyaphobia:** fear the top of the airline will suddenly rip open and I will be sucked out at forty thousand feet over the Pacific while strapped to a two-hundred pound metal object, my seat.
- **Slyaphobia:** fear that the movie on a flight to the West Coast will be a *Rocky*.
- **Gimmethataphobia:** fear of, in the unlikely event of cabin depressurization, my oxygen mask will work, but not the one

belonging to the guy sitting next to me, and he will be Buster Douglas.

- *Ebony*aphobia: fear that all my favorite magazines will have been taken by other passengers and all I've got left to read is *Ebony*.
- **Baitaphobia:** even worse, all that's left to read is *Field and Stream*.
- **Bornagainaphobia:** fear of being seated next to a religious nut with a lot of pamphlets.
- **Fruitoftheloomaphobia:** fear the pilot's underwear is too tight and he's paying more attention to that than all those little dials in front of him.

The good news is now you can forget about **Virginiaslimaphobia:** the fear of breathing secondhand smoke in an airplane.

The bad news is now there's the fear of getting too much cosmic radiation while you're flying: **Flashgordonaphobia.**

Flights of Fright

The Supreme Court has been asked to decide whether or not airline passengers can sue for damages if they've had the devil scared out of them on a flight.

The case involves passengers on an Eastern flight from Miami to Nassau in 1983. The plane eventually lost all its engines, and passengers were told they could crash in the Atlantic.

One engine did start up again, however, and the plane was able to land back to Miami.

A lawyer for the passengers said his clients were terrorized and many had suffered psychic damages; some would not be able to fly again.

I am keeping a keen eye on this matter.

If the court were to rule in favor of the passengers, it could mean I soon will come into a large sum of money.

I get the devil scared out of me every time I fly, and it's the airlines' fault. They should realize it doesn't make any sense that those big things can get up in the air and stay there; and intelligent people like myself know that and therefore are quite apprehensive the moment we step onto an airline.

(It would also follow, I suppose, that if we're so intelligent, why do we get on a plane in the first place? Well, ever try to get from Atlanta to Omaha on Amtrak?)

I am frightened the most during takeoffs and landings.

First, you've got to get the plane in the air. If that happens, then you've still got to figure out a way to get it back on the ground again.

I've never understood why the flight attendants take my drink away during both takeoffs and landings.

"I'm sorry, sir," they say, "but we're about to take off [or land], and I'll have to take your drink."

That's when I need a drink the most. They ought to announce to all the passengers, "We're about to take off [or land] so we'll be passing out drinks."

I'm a little better once the plane levels off and the seat-belt sign goes off, indicating it is safe for me to get up and move about the cabin as I wish.

But what about the unlikely event of cabin depressurization?

Will my oxygen mask actually fall down in front of my face? Will I be able to figure out how to place it over my nose and mouth and continue to breathe normally before I die?

And what if my seat cushion won't float? The plane goes down in some farm pond and there I am trying to paddle to the bank on my seat cushion and it won't float like they promised me it would.

Maybe one of the farmer's pigs will swim out and rescue me. But can pigs swim?

Any change in engine sound terrifies me when I fly. And when they start monkeying around with the flaps and landing gear, it sounds like the tail just fell off.

I'm even frightened by other passengers. Ever notice that on every flight you take, there's always at least one guy sitting near you who looks like an Arab terrorist?

He's the one with all the hair who's down on his knees in the aisle chanting.

The truth is, everybody should be at least a little nervous when they fly. If for no other reason, here's one:

How much did the cockpit crew have to drink the night before in the hotel lounge?

See what I mean?

I've got a call in to my lawyer now.

Packaged for Air Safety . . . That's a Wrap

I have a friend who is just as afraid and skeptical of flying as I am. We both have overcome those fears to the point we will, in fact, get into an airplane if there is no other recourse and there is an ample supply of bottled courage aboard.

My friend made a great point recently.

"I was flying the other day," she began, "and it occurred to me. You know the safest planes to fly?"

I didn't.

"Those planes that deliver packages," she said. "Like Federal Express and UPS. You never hear of those planes crashing and scattering packages all over the ground. They ought to sell seats on those planes. I wouldn't mind sharing my space with a package or two."

She's right, you know. It may be just that I am more sensitive to airline disasters than most others, but haven't there been a lot of plane crashes lately?

And it's always people getting scattered all over the ground, not packages.

Are airlines that carry packages more careful than airlines that carry people?

"Hey, Harvey, check that fuel line?"

"Nah, Carl. Not that many passengers going out tonight. I'll catch it next week."

So what do they say over at Fed Ex?

"Checked it twice, Carl. Got some pretty important packages going up tonight."

I guess the thing about people is if you scatter one of them over the ground, they aren't that hard to find. You might not be able to identify them right away, but at least you can find a person.

Not the same with a package. It could be a tiny package, and if the plane crashed, it might never be found and it might be somebody's new wristwatch being shipped as a birthday present.

I realize this sounds terribly callous, and I'm not really saying packages are more important to airlines than passengers, but maybe the safest way to fly is to send yourself inside a package.

"Federal Express?"

"Yes."

"I'd like to send a package to Cleveland."

"How big a package?"

"Pretty big one."

"How big?"

"How's six-one sound?"

"Six feet one inch tall?"

"Yeah. My mother's people were all over six feet."

"Are you implying you'd like to send yourself in a package?"

"Just to Cleveland. I've got an important meeting there."

"Sorry to pry, sir, but why don't you consider booking a flight on a passenger carrier?"

"I'd rather go with you guys. You never crash and scatter packages all over the ground, do you?"

"Well, of course not, but . . ."

"Then tell me what time to show up, and I'll get inside a big box and I'll be fine."

"You can't smoke."

"I won't."

"Okay, if you're willing to try. Will this be first class or tourist?"

"What's the difference?"

"In first class, the air holes we punch in the top of your box are complimentary."

The Bus Way to Travel

This column is coming to you today from a bus. I'm not talking Winnebago here. I'm talking bus, as in a great big, large Greyhound, John Madden bus. You could put the entire tenor section of the Mormon Tabernacle Choir on this bus and there would still be room to store all the robes in the back.

Allow me to tell you how I came about this bus:

I travel approximately 120 days a year, and I've been doing that for ten years. Mostly I travel to speaking engagements. The money's good, and I get to tell a lot of jokes.

That, of course, has involved a great deal of flying. I have more frequent-flyer points than Peter Pan. What am I going to use them for? To take a trip?

Here's the problem with flying these days. There are no more late-night flights. Let's say I have a speaking engagement in Baton Rouge.

I fly in, do my dog-and-pony thing, and now it's ten o'clock at night, and there's no way back to Atlanta until the first flight the next morning.

The plane, of course, is an hour late taking off. I've got to wait for my bags at the airport, and by the time I finally get back home, it's already afternoon. I'm tired and frazzled from the flight, the day's shot, and all I want to do is get in bed and watch terrible cable movies starring John Candy, which is redundant.

Then, I came up with the bus idea. I lease the big sucker out of Nashville. The bus picks me up the night before Baton Rouge.

The driver—a nice guy named Sonny, who even looks a little like John Candy but probably is a better actor—drives through the night to Baton Rouge while I'm in the back in a double bed, sleeping babylike to the drone of the engine.

I do the speech. At ten that evening, I'm back on the bus, enjoying a cold beverage as we head home.

I awaken fresh the next morning in front of my home, and Sonny takes my bags in for me and I've got the entire day.

There are a couple of problems involving the bus. One is, it's—well—a little tacky: There is a painting of wild horses on the side. I arrive in my neighborhood at seven in the morning and my neighbors see a giant bus with wild horses on the side and I'm certain they have immediate concerns about a drop in their property values.

The other problem is that when the bus is stopped, people want to know who's inside it.

They've actually opened the door, looked inside, and said, "Who's in there? Willie Nelson?"

I say, "Yeah, Willie's in the back writing a song. I'm Buford on rhythm guitar."

If there is a point here, it's that, in 1990, it's more convenient to take a bus than a commercial airplane.

You're hassle-free, you don't have to wait for anybody to get out of the rest room, there's no turbulence, or any air-traffic controller to put you on the wrong runway so you run into another plane.

All that says to me is that ground transportation, rapid and convenient, may be the thing of the future, and we will have come the full transportation cycle.

My next move is to put together a leveraged buy-out of Eastern Airlines, knock the wings off the planes and use them for chartered buses.

By the way, Sonny, pull over here and let's get a cheeseburger. Try that on your next flight.

9 WHAT <u>ARE</u> THEY WEARING?

I consider myself an expert on women's fashion. With three ex-wives, I've bought enough female garb to clothe the entire University of New Hampshire field-hockey team, if the University of New Hampshire has such a thing.

Cheek Out
Moon Britches

Did you read the story about Moon Britches? It was in all the papers.

A guy out of Texas has come up with the idea of selling shorts and slacks with a zipper in the back to make mooning—the showing of one's bare hindparts to others for the sheer rascality involved or as a means of expressing dislike, anger, or belittlement—more convenient.

The designer, Richard Cottrell, predicts mooning will be a popular activity in the nineties, as in, "Show Your Hiney in '90."

In the past, in order to moon someone it was necessary to strip from the waist down to your knees.

With a pair of Moon Britches on, all that would be necessary is simply turning your back toward your target and unzipping the back zipper.

(I guess what else would be necessary would be not to wear any underclothing, but let's don't get into that.)

Let's say you are at a stoplight and your high school principal is sitting in the car next to you, a classical mooning opportunity.

Before Moon Britches, you might not have the time to get into the mooning mode before the light changed and your principal drove unmooned.

With Moon Britches, however, it would take only a matter of seconds to fire. So what if the principal also got a glimpse of your face and suspended you from school? You'll be a hero to the other guys in shop class when you're reinstated.

(I once knew a guy who was so ugly he stuck his face out a car window and was arrested for mooning.)

I'm not certain how I feel about all this. I, of course, have never taken part in such a sophomoric, somewhat antisocial, stunt. I was raised to know better.

However, I have been the target of a mooner, and I have known others who have gotten mooning down to a science.

I was driving down a lonely stretch of interstate highway one day, and a carload of young women drove up next to me and the one in the front seat on the passenger side shot and hit.

I was appalled.

"Do it again!" I screamed out my window.

I had a friend who was a regular mooning fool back in high school. Among his many scores were the girls' choir, the cafeteria staff, fifth-period study hall, and his mother's Tupperware party.

My basic concern with Moon Britches is that because of their convenience and stated purpose they will cause mooning to become commonplace, the result being that mooning will lose a lot of its effect. You could get mooned four times driving to McDonald's. People who work in the drive-in window could get mooned all day. They would become so bored they would simply reply, "Want some french fries with that?"

In my mind mooning should be a spontaneous gesture. It should also be a rare occurrence. And it should take a little effort, which Moon Britches basically make unnecessary.

I say serious mooners should stick with the old method and let Moon Britches die a swift death and take oat bran with them.

Incidentally, who else my friend from high school mooned included the chief of police, a Greyhound bus filled with passengers, and a monthly meeting of the United Daughters of the Confederacy.

He grew up to be an astronaut.

When You
Gotta Go . . .

A reader mailed me a clip of a story about a woman inventing a new type of pants for women that makes it easier for them, well, to relieve themselves.

You see, if a woman happens to be wearing a pair of pants—and there are a lot of women wearing them these days—it is sort of inconvenient and time-consuming for them when nature calls.

Take a woman police officer, for instance. While her male counterpart simply can unzip, the woman must remove her pants and her gunbelt and her radio and whatever else she is packing around her waist, and that's a big hassle.

First, however, what I've been trying to figure out is why the reader sent me this particular clipping.

Was it because of my ill-deserved reputation as a sexist? Did the reader think this fashion development was funny? Did this person want my thoughts on this development?

Whatever the reason was, allow me to say that this is a bit of a sticky subject, and I will attempt to handle it with all the dignity and care I can muster.

And as far as being sexist is concerned, let me also say that I think it only fair for women to be able to relieve themselves with the same ease as a man, while wearing pants, and I even think women can look quite attractive in pants as long as they aren't baggy.

Putting a pair of baggy pants on a woman would be like pulling a shade down over a lovely sunset. (Is that sexist? I was just trying to pay a compliment here.)

There is nothing funny about this. It's an important issue.

Here's what the article said:

A lady named Carolyn Stradley, president of a paving company, has designed "The Equalizers."

According to the article, "The . . . design has a zippered seam which extends from just below the waistband at the back of the pants downward through the seat portion and crotch area and up to the waistband at the front.

"The pants also include integrated fleece-lined underpants which use the same releasable seam design."

Ms. Stradley was quoted as saying, "These pants are designed in such a manner that you do not have to bare your buttocks or your bottom torso, and you have complete access to relieve yourself."

The article also pointed out that more and more women are getting into pants-wearing work, and included an incredible statistic that by the year 2000 women will comprise 47.5 percent of all construction workers, and that's a lot of hard-hatted Hannahs.

As I mentioned earlier, I think it only fair women get a break like this, and I would also like to mention that anything that might contribute to cutting down on the time it takes a woman to use the rest room is long overdue.

"I want it to go," said Ms. Stradley. "I want it to be the next Coca-Cola."

As author of the acclaimed tome *When My Love Returns from the Ladies Room, Will I Be Too Old to Care?* so, by golly, do I.

And if that's a sexist statement, then so be it. When you gotta go, you gotta go, and sometimes a man has just gotta say what he's gotta say.

Women in Running Shoes Brought to Heel

WASHINGTON—My ride was late, so as I waited on the sidewalk in downtown Washington, I people-watched.

I had seen the phenomenon I'm about to discuss in other large cities, but here in Washington there seem to be more instances of it. I'm speaking of the fact that when females in the workplace are out of their offices, many are now walking around in their otherwise-attractive outfits in running shoes.

I am told that women wear these shoes to and from work and when they go to lunch, but once they are in their offices, they put on regular shoes, ones with heels that are more suited to the rest of their clothing.

I asked a female colleague about this once, and she explained, "We do it for comfort. You just can't imagine how doing a lot of walking in heels can absolutely kill your feet."

I can understand that. I've never personally done a lot of walking (or any walking, for that matter) in a pair of heels, but I can imagine how one's feet would feel afterward.

Still, I've got to say this:

Comfort or no comfort, wearing a pair of running shoes with a dress does to the attractiveness of a woman what a large tattoo does to a man.

It's downright displeasing to the eye. In a word—ugly.

And I hate to use the T-word, but I feel compelled.

It's Tacky.

At a gathering later in the evening I asked a Washington woman, who had had the good sense not to show up at a cocktail party wearing a pair of Reeboks, why this practice seemed so prevalent in Washington.

"I don't think it has anything to do with politics," she said. "Maybe Washington women just have to walk more than women in other cities. Why do you ask?"

Diplomacy has never been my strong suit. I looked at her square in her eyes and said, "Because it's tacky."

She threw a sausage ball at me and then huffed away in disgust.

But that didn't change my opinion. I don't think I have any sort of foot fetish, but women in sexy shoes have always caught my eye.

I recall the first time I saw Kathy Sue Loudermilk in a pair of high heels. It was at the annual Moreland Fourth of July barbecue. She was also wearing her tight pink sweater (the one they retired in the trophy case when she graduated from high school), a pair of short shorts, and eight-inch spike heels.

When the preacher, who was helping make the coleslaw, saw her, he said, "Lord, Thou dost make some lovely things."

I don't think he was talking about the cabbage he was putting in the coleslaw.

Said my boyhood friend and idol, Weyman C. Wannamaker, Jr., a great American, when he saw Kathy Sue, "You put something besides them heels on that body, and you done put retreads on a Rolls-Royce."

And here I stand on a downtown sidewalk in our nation's capital, and eight out of ten women I see look like they went to the Sears tire store to shop for shoes.

The Lord does, indeed, make some lovely things, and I'm certain the Almighty had no intention they walk around in what amounts to glorified, overpriced, rubber-soled clodhoppers.

Your feet hurt, ladies? See Dr. Scholl.

Tacky. Tacky. Tacky.

I think I have made myself abundantly clear.

 10 BRINGING UP BABY

I don't have any children of my own.
I'm afraid if I had a son, he would come
home wearing an earring and announce
he wanted to attend Georgia Tech.

The Name's
the Game

From a UCLA psychology professor comes a new book titled *The Name Game: The Decision That Lasts a Lifetime.* It is published by National Press Books and will cost you $9.95 to have a copy of your very own.

I read about the book in my local newspaper, which costs me a quarter. These are tough times.

According to the report, Dr. Albert Mehrabian, the author, says children are often given names on a whim, instinct, family tradition, or as attempted humor.

Says Dr. Mehrabian: "You owe it to your children to select a name that will help them get through life and not handicap them."

Having a child soon?

What name should you select for the addition to the family that will help the little darling get through life without a handicap such as being named "Norbert" or "Ernestine"?

In his book Dr. Mehrabian offers the following names as the ones that best say, "This person is a success."

FOR GIRLS: 1. Jacqueline 2. Katherine 3. Samantha 4. Victoria 5. Lauren

FOR BOYS: 1. James 2. Madison 3. Charles 4. Alexander 5. Kenneth

I can go along with these. There're Jacqueline(s) Bisset and Onassis. And, of course, Lauren Bacall.

Samantha Farnsworth won back-to-back Miss Collard Festival titles back home. Then there's Queen Victoria, Victoria Principal, and Victoria Station.

For boys there's Jesse James, who was a successful bank and train robber before he turned his back.

There're Prince Charles, Alexander the Great (no relation to Catherine), and my cousin Kenneth, a successful hunter and fisherman who showed me how to throw a curveball when I was eight.

I've never had any children of my own to name, but if I ever do, I want to take Dr. Mehrabian's advice and be very careful.

Here are some names I would avoid if I had a son: Norbert, Gunther, Seymour, Pig Face, Clarence, Spiro, Sammy Joe Bob, Running Buffalo, or Gilroy.

For girls I'd stay away from Ernestine, Willamena, Clovis, Mavis, Nanci Jo, Anna Sue, Gourd Head, Darting Squirrel, or Oprylandria.

You are asking, "Oprylandria?"

I have a friend who is a teacher, and she swears there was a little girl in her class named Oprylandria.

When she asked the parents why such a name, they said it was because the child was conceived during a visit to Opryland. A sick attempt at humor, indeed.

God help the child if her parents had been visiting Little Rock.

I'm fairly satisfied with my own name, Lewis. That was my father's name, too, and he got it from his maternal grandfather.

It's no "James" or "Madison" or "Alexander," but my mother explained to me I was conceived in 1945 in a sleeping berth on a train.

So, had my own parents had the weird sense of humor of little Oprylandria's parents, I could have been named "Coal Car," "Sidetrack," or "Three Hours Late."

Another one of my cousins, "Motel 6," is a story I'll get to at another time.

Be Up to Date While Bringing Up Baby

My friend Rigsby, the brand-new father, is very proud of his first child. She's only three weeks old.

"It's been quite an experience being a father for the first time," said Rigsby.

"But doesn't your wife do everything that needs to be done for the baby?" I asked.

"These are the nineties, you Neanderthal," said Rigsby. "The husband and the wife now share the duties that only the poor wife handled back in the Dark Ages."

This gave me an idea. There must be a lot of new first-time fathers out there who are sensitive like Rigsby and want to share in the caring of the baby.

Mothers, of course, are born knowing how to get a baby through its newborn period—like they are born knowing when to begin force-feeding their children liver after they are old enough to chew.

"But men," Rigsby explained, "learn mostly by trial and error."

I asked if he would offer a guide for first-time fathers. This column always has stood for offering a public service whenever possible.

"Start with diapers," I suggested to Rigsby.

"First of all," he said, "diaper technology has come a long way since safety pins and cloth.

"Believe it or not, a wet diaper doesn't feel wet anymore. They hide the water now in a secret compartment in the diaper.

"The way you know it's time to change the diaper is, if it weighed less than an ounce when you put it on baby and has suddenly become heavier than your bowling ball, it's time for a change.

"In general, however, if it's been more than five minutes since you put the diaper on, it's probably time to apply a new one."

"How about bottle feeding?" I asked.

"What you have to worry about is getting a nipple with too big a hole," said Rigsby. "If that happens, your baby does not get enough of a sucking workout and might grow up to have a difficult time eating spaghetti."

"What do you mean by that?" I asked.

"You know when you're eating spaghetti and you lose control of the noodles and they're sort of just hanging there on your chin and you have to suck them into your mouth before anybody sees you? Well, if a baby doesn't get a good sucking workout, it might lead to a great deal of embarrassment in the future."

Makes sense to me. I asked about babies burping.

"After an ounce or two of whatever you are feeding the baby," Rigsby explained, "the gas monster will strike."

"You mean a baby can make a loud burping sound?"

"Remember John Belushi in *Animal House?* A tiny baby could match burps with him any day."

"What else?" I asked.

"Poop," said Rigsby.

"Poop?" I asked.

"Yes, poop," he answered. "You can't talk about babies without talking a little poop."

"Just be careful," I warned him.

"First," he began, "don't be alarmed by poop color changes. Most earth tones, including green and Day-Glo orange, are in the normal range.

"Second, there's one thing the new diaper technology has not covered yet, and that is they haven't found a secret compartment in the diaper for the poop yet, and since poop spreads faster than an Exxon spill . . ."

"That's enough," I said, adding, "You haven't said anything about getting up in the middle of the night when the baby cries."

"That's not my job," he explained. "The little woman handles that one."

Gift Ideas for Today's Teenagers

I hear a lot of my male friends complaining because they don't know what to give their children for Christmas.

Allow me to clarify that. The men I hear complaining the most are the ones with teenaged children. Those with younger offspring appear to have it much easier.

They buy their kids Nintendo games and dolls that file sex-discrimination suits. These seem to have replaced the toy truck and Barbie.

But what do you give the teenager on the brink of the nineties? I would really like to help these people, but my credibility in this area, I admit, is somewhat suspect since I don't have any children, teenaged or otherwise.

However, as an observer of life in all its phases, perhaps an outsider like myself can, in fact, select appropriate gifts for teenagers even better than their parents can.

I have already admitted I am not a parent, but I did have some. And in the immortal words of my mother, "Believe it or not, I was a teenager myself once, and I don't care if you are sixteen, you're not getting a Corvette for Christmas."

In other words, I think I can understand both points of view, thereby giving me an edge over parents whose minds are cluttered by such thoughts as, If I give my kid a Corvette for Christmas, will he (or she) drive it through a K mart?

Here are some gift ideas for teenage boys:

- An earring: Earrings have become quite popular with teenaged boys. I realize most fathers likely can't stand the thought of their sons wearing an earring, but they're cheaper than a Corvette and he's already dyed his hair orange.
- A guitar: What do you think you give a kid who wears an earring and dyes his hair orange? A set of golf clubs?
- A motorcycle: Maybe he'll drive it through a K mart and get sent to reform school. You can tell your friends at the club your son has joined the marines.
- A face-lift: As soon as a kid dyes his hair orange, starts wearing an earring, and joins a rock group, the term "zit-head" takes on an entire new meaning.
- A box of condoms: Believe it or not, some chicks go for zit-heads.

Now for your teenaged daughter:

- Tight-fitting jeans: Daddy's little girl has grown up. Plus, all the other girls are wearing them.
- A pair of red high heels to wear with her tight-fitting jeans: What, you wanted to give her a chastity belt?
- A convertible: Perhaps she'll drive it through a Neiman-Marcus and get sent to girls' reform school, where she'll be safe. You can tell your friends at the club your daughter has become a nun.
- A trip to Europe: in case the convertible thing doesn't work. Maybe while she's gone, she'll forget about that zit-head she's been dating.
- A box of condoms: in case she doesn't.

11 THERE'S JUST SOME THINGS THAT AIN'T FIT TO EAT

All you've ever wanted to know, and a few things you probably didn't, about certain edible items, like white soup beans, oat bran and cheeseburgers, hold the soybeans.

Resolutions, Southern Style

I can pride myself on two major accomplishments in 1990. Both have to do with my fondness for down-home Southern cooking.

I favor down-home Southern cooking because I am from a down-home Southern home. That, and it tastes good.

I want my chicken fried, my steak with gravy, my green beans cooked, and my tomatoes served raw.

Too many fancy restaurants serve their green beans raw and then they cook their tomatoes—and give you some sort of hard, dark bread with it. This is an unholy aberration I cannot abide.

I find the best down-home Southern cooking at a small restaurant in Atlanta, which features fried chicken, country-fried steak, meat loaf, and, on Fridays, beef tips on rice and home-cooked vegetables—and uncooked tomatoes, of course.

Imagine my shock, however, when I went to order my vegetables one day and the list on the menu included "Northern beans."

"There must be some mistake," I said to my favorite waitress, Jo. "This says, 'Northern beans.' How can you list Northern beans in a down-home Southern cooking place?"

"What do you call them?" asked Jo.

" 'White soup beans,' of course," I answered.

My mother used to cook white soup beans for me.

It's a little-known fact, but when Jesus fed the masses, he served white soup beans with the fish and bread. "Northern" beans aren't mentioned anywhere in the Bible.

Jo said, "I'll see what I can do."

I come in a week later, and it says "White soup beans" on the menu. Praise Him.

Accomplishment No. 1.

Another place I often eat is at a golf club in Atlanta, which has good chili.

Chili is down home as long as you don't put any mushrooms in it. They serve corn bread with the down-home chili at the club.

The problem is, the corn bread is sweet. Corn bread is not supposed to be sweet. That's in the Bible, too. The Book of Martha White, 7:11.

If you want something sweet, order the pound cake. Anybody who puts sugar in the corn bread is a heathen who doesn't love the Lord, not to mention Southeastern Conference football.

Anyway, in late December I went to the club and ordered the chili.

"You ought to try the corn bread," said the waiter. "The chef got tired of you complaining, so he quit putting sugar in it."

I tasted the corn bread. No sugar. I called out the chef.

"Verily," I said unto him, "it's about time you stopped making a sacrilege out of corn bread."

Accomplishment No. 2.

I feel so good about my two feats of 1990, I've got two new targets for '91.

I'm going to see if I can convince fast-food places to start cutting up their own french fries instead of using frozen ones, and I'm going to see if I can help white bread make a comeback in this country.

Do not underestimate me. I'm on a mission from God.

Ex—Health Nut Breaks for Breakfast

My friend Rigsby, the health nut, had that look in his eye.

"I did it," he said.

"Did what?" I asked him.

"I had breakfast."

"So did I," I said. "What's the big deal?"

"I had a real breakfast," Rigsby answered. "For ten years all I've had for breakfast are things that are supposed to be good for me.

"I've eaten enough oat bran to qualify for the Kentucky Derby. I've eaten more yogurt than a hundred-and-twelve-year-old Russian. I've eaten so many bananas on my granola, I'm growing hair on my back and twice a day have a serious urge to go hang upside down on a tree limb."

"But breakfast is our most important meal," I said. "You should be eating healthy in the morning."

"I don't care," said Rigsby. "Man can't live on fiber alone. He must also have an occasional scrambled egg."

"You ate an egg?" I asked him in disbelief.

"Four," Rigsby answered.

I don't remember the last time I had an egg. I think it was during the Eisenhower administration.

"Aren't you afraid of getting too much cholesterol?" I asked Rigsby.

"I've got to die of something, and if an egg doesn't get me, something else will."

"What else did you have?"

"A Belgian waffle," said Rigsby. "With butter and syrup all over it."

"That's a lot of sugar. What about hypoglycemia?"

"What about it?"

"Well," I attempted to explain, "you could become faint, disoriented, and develop diabetes."

"Yeah," said Rigsby. "I also could get run over by a beer truck, but I'm still going to cross the street."

"Did you eat anything else?"

"I had some bacon."

"Bacon, studies show, can cause cancer."

"And I ate some white toast."

"No nutritional value there. You should have eaten whole wheat."

"And some pancakes."

"On top of the Belgian waffle? Are your affairs in order?"

"And some hash-brown potatoes."

"All that grease. Who's the executor of your will?"

"And three chocolate doughnuts."

"You won't live until Christmas."

"And some leftover pizza from the night before."

"Our Father, who art . . ."

"And a Little Debbie Snack Cake."

"We're going to miss you."

"And a pot of coffee."

"Decaf, of course."

"High test."

"I'm looking at a dead man."

"And you know what else?" Rigsby asked me.

"What else?"

"I'm going to do it again in the morning."

It takes a real man, I suppose, to stare death square in the eye. I think I'll go over to the Waffle House and drool.

Would a Stomach Pump Help?

I had a gastronomic disorder recently. Christmas and gastronomic disorders seem to go hand in hand.

This one put me to bed for thirty-six hours with stomach pains and various accompanying miseries.

All I could do was just lie there and watch an Elizabeth Taylor film festival on one of the cable stations as I tried to determine what caused my stomach to hurt like it did.

"Obviously, it was something I ate or drank," I said to myself.

Let's see. There was the Christmas party Saturday night with a nice bartender who asked me every eight seconds, "Could I freshen that up a bit for you?"

The reason he could ask me that is because I was never out of pouring distance from him for any period longer than eight seconds.

But that couldn't have been what made me sick. I'm too old to get sick from drinking too much at a party. I haven't thrown up from drinking since that unfortunate occurrence during my sophomore year in college that resulted in the heavy laundry bill for my date.

Perhaps it was the ice. That had to be it. Bad ice. Probably made out of tap water that didn't have one of those little filters on it that Paul Harvey is always talking about.

Then maybe it was something I ate at the party? Let's see, I started with the little sausages, moved to the chicken wings, and then dallied for a time with the shrimp.

I followed that up with the smoked oysters and cheese, cake, pie, brownies, and a stick of butter.

But it couldn't have been something I ate that made me sick, because I didn't have but nine of the Swedish meatballs.

Maybe, on the other hand, it's just a virus going around. That's got to be it. Probably Bush brought it back from Malta.

Wait. Didn't I go to a Christmas brunch Sunday morning? I did. But I only had eight Bloody Marys, and I just tasted my bacon-cheese-tomato-onion-mushroom-sardine-Hershey-bar omelet.

Okay, so I ate the whole thing. And a waffle.

But that couldn't have made me sick. I washed the whole thing down with some champagne, and everybody knows champagne has all those bubbles that are good for your stomach.

Perhaps it was what I found in the back of the refrigerator—the beer and pretzels and popcorn and cheese puffs and nachos and the bean dip me and the guys had Sunday afternoon watching the football games.

Is bean dip supposed to have all that green stuff on the top of it?

But nobody else got sick. Harvey had to have his stomach pumped later that night, but he figures it was due to the fact he dropped the mortgage payment taking the Chicago Bears.

And all I had before bedtime Sunday night was a quart of ice cream and what was left of the nachos and a fish-stick sandwich, so that couldn't have been it, either.

It had to be bad ice.

A dozen Tagamets, a jar of Maalox, three packages of Pepto-Bismol tablets, and every Elizabeth Taylor movie from *Ivanhoe* to *Butterfield 8* later, I had my answer.

Body Language

My body and I had a long talk the other morning.

First, my heart asked, "What's that you're drinking?"

"Coffee," I said, adding, with some degree of pride, "but it's decaffeinated. Caffeine is bad for me, so I've cut it out."

"Uh-oh," said my heart.

"What do you mean?" I asked.

"You haven't heard," replied my heart. "A new study has indicated decaffeinated coffee is made from beans that can cause bad cholesterol. You keep drinking that stuff, and my arteries will clog up and we'll buy the farm."

I already had cut down on eggs to help reduce my cholesterol count. Now, I'm told decaffeinated coffee, which I thought was good for me, picks up where the eggs leave off.

"One other thing," said my heart, "you know how you often get up in the middle of the night and go downstairs and eat some raw zucchini?"

"Raw vegetables are good for me," I said.

"That may very well be," said my heart, "but another new study says getting up suddenly in the middle of the night can cause a heart attack."

"So no more midnight raw zucchini?"

"No more," said my heart.

My colon piped up.

"What's that you're eating?" it asked.

"Cereal," I said. "I'm doing it for you."

"What's that cereal made from?"

"Healthy grains of corn, I suppose," I answered.

"Uh-oh," said my colon.

"What's the problem?"

"You should be eating cereal made from oat bran. It's better for me than what you're eating now."

"Who says?" I asked my colon.

"The people who sell oat bran."

I was getting discouraged.

My blood joined in.

"You're not actually going to eat that cinnamon roll, are you?"

"I love cinnamon rolls," I answered. "What's wrong with a cinnamon roll?"

"Sugar," said my blood. "Eat too much sugar and we'll have to deal with hypoglycemia."

"Dang right," said my pancreas.

"But I drink diet soft drinks, to cut down on my sugar intake," I said.

"Yeah," my blood said. "You and all those dead laboratory rats."

Just then my stomach joined in the conversation.

"Since eating fish can prevent cancer, when am I going to get some more fish?" asked my stomach.

"I'm afraid to eat any more fish," I said. "I saw a report on television saying to be careful about eating fish because the government wasn't doing a very good job inspecting it and I could get hepatitis."

"Big deal. You want me to get cancer?" my stomach asked.

After that, I made a few decisions.

I decided I wouldn't drink any sort of coffee anymore, I'd eat cereals made only of oat bran, I'd cut out all sugars—both real and artificial—I'd call in twelve government inspectors to look over any fish I was about to eat, and I would never, under any circumstances, get up at midnight, which could cause me to have a heart attack.

(If my house catches on fire at midnight, I'll cross that bridge when I come to it.)

Then I thought, What if I do all that and radon gas seeps into my house and kills me?

I went to the refrigerator, pulled out a nonalcoholic beer, and had myself a good cry.

Oat Bran-ded
a Fad

I am very proud of myself for never eating a single ounce of oat bran during the "Great Oat Bran Crusade." That is, I didn't eat any oat bran unless somebody slipped in a spoonful in one of my daily cheeseburgers.

The primary reason I didn't eat any oat bran, other than the fact I firmly believe oats are for horses and ground chuck is for people, is I am sick and tired of being told what I should and shouldn't eat.

What you eat, I firmly believe, is nobody else's business but your own.

These feelings go back to childhood.

Childhood is a difficult time because mothers are always on constant what-food-is-good-for-you patrol.

In my house it was liver. My mother served liver about once every two weeks.

The first time I ever saw liver on my plate, I knew I didn't like it.

"How do you know you aren't going to like it if you haven't tried it?" my mother, and about ten billion other mothers, would say.

I just knew, that's all. I don't have to try aluminum siding first before I know for a fact I don't like it. And the same went for liver.

"But liver is good for you," my mother would say next.

I didn't care. I didn't care if the fact I wouldn't eat liver would cut my life span in half. I reasoned I'd rather live a few good years liverless than a full lifetime of trying to get it down my gullet.

Teachers also told me what I should eat. My second-grade teacher wouldn't allow any members of her class to leave the lunchroom until their plates were completely clean.

This meant I was faced with the hard situation of having to eat English peas, which they served in school lunchrooms about three times a week.

I hated English peas. I still hate English peas, and I hate anybody who doesn't.

I didn't hate English peas as much as I did liver, but they were a close second.

At some point during the second grade, I went on an English pea strike. Gandhi would have been proud.

I simply said to myself, "I'm not going to eat one more English pea even if it means I have to sit in this lunchroom until I'm thirty-five, which is probably when I'll die anyway since I don't eat liver."

School officials finally called in federal arbitrators to mediate the dispute. After hearing all the testimony, and sampling some of the English peas themselves, the arbitrators ruled if I would agreed to eat chalk three times a week, I couldn't be forced to eat English peas, too. At least chalk was crunchy.

I smelled a laboratory rat in the oat-bran thing from the very start. As soon as somebody said oat bran is helpful in reducing cholesterol, there were more oat-bran commercials on television than laundry-detergent commercials.

Any day I expected to see a commercial that said, "Tide. The only laundry detergent with oat bran."

But now a study published in the *New England Journal of Medicine* has shown that oat bran has no special cholesterol-lowering benefit. Oat bran, the study concluded, was "over-hyped."

Oat bran as it turns out, may have been just another health-food fad that made a lot of people a lot of bucks.

The next time another hype like that comes along, do like me, and just say no. It's the right thing to do.

Up the Creek with Bottled Water

They found out some bottles of Perrier had benzene in them, and now Perrier drinkers are afraid to drink the stuff. Ha. Ha. Ha.

I'm laughing because I think Perrier is stupid and anybody who drinks Perrier is stupid.

You know what Perrier is? It's water that bubbles out of a spring in France somewhere. I've seen people—usually in their twenties and thirties who spend their weekends biking around in their tight biking britches—go into those fancy bars and order Perrier for $3.50 a pop.

They apparently think Perrier, since it's from France and comes in a bottle, is better for them than regular American water that comes out of a regular American tap.

And some of these people order Perrier on the rocks, which is water over ice, and the ice is made from, you guessed it, tap water. These people ride tricycles.

My late father was one of the great ice-water drinkers of all time. He drank a lot of other stuff, too, which is perhaps why he was always thirsty for ice water.

Anyway, whenever he stopped for gasoline, he would ask the station attendant, "Do you have any ice water?"

One day, we stopped and my father asked for ice water, and the attendant brought it out and said, "That'll be a dime."

"You're charging me for ice water?" my father asked, shocked beyond belief.

He gave the water back to the man, called him a communist son-of-a-pig, and off we drove.

Can you imagine what my father would have thought about people paying $3.50 for a glass of water in one of those bars where the guys all wear suspenders?

Water used to be simple. There was well water. You just dug a hole on your property until you hit water.

Your Ol' Uncle Lewis here can remember getting a drink of water by lowering a bucket into the well with a rope.

Well water was always cold, never made anybody sick that I know of, and it was free.

Ol' Uncle Lewis also can remember when you could drink water out of a creek. There was a creek on Red Murphy's property, and what a creek it was.

Because there were no Nintendo games or crack, we used to dam the creek about twice a week for fun and to get high.

The creek was fed by a spring. If you got thirsty while damming the creek, you went over to the spring, got down on your belly, stuck your mouth to the water, and drank your fill.

There are still springs, but I wouldn't drink out of any of them anymore. If there's not benzene floating around, there's probably worse.

My premise here is that although there might be some chemicals in your tap water, it must still be safe to drink, given all the modern purifying techniques of city waterworks.

And to pay some ridiculous price for a bottle of water shipped all the way from France by people you don't even know is, well, like I said earlier, stupid—benzene or no benzene.

By the way, if you are now, or have ever been before, a Perrier drinker, you may have some benzene in you.

Know what benzene causes? It causes your butt to get huge so it won't fit into your tight bike britches anymore.

Ha. Ha. Ha.

Never Give a Cheeseburger to a Communist

If you are reading this anywhere but in school, you ought to bow your head for a moment and give thanks for the wonderful news that came out this week.

Cheeseburgers, in case you didn't hear, may not be bad for you after all. In fact, they could actually be beneficial to your health.

Some California scientists fed some cheeseburgers to some mice and found out there are chemicals in well-done burgers and cheese that fight stomach tumors in the little critters.

If cheeseburgers help mice, they may also help people, and people eat a lot more cheeseburgers than mice, and I eat more cheeseburgers than most people, so praise the Lord and pass the french fries.

I've probably averaged eating four cheeseburgers a week for my entire adult life.

I eat a lot of cheeseburgers for a couple of reasons. One, they are greasy and they taste good.

Two, I have a standard rule when eating in a restaurant I'm not familiar with: It's hard to screw up a cheeseburger, so whenever I'm in doubt, that's usually what I order.

Can anybody recall when there was a scientific study that indicated something that tastes good might also be good for you?

I can't. In fact, I adhere to the thoughts of a wise man who once offered the following lament: "Everything I like is immoral, illegal, or fattening." Add "detrimental to my health" to that, and we have a dilemma so familiar to those of us living on the brink of the twenty-first century.

Naturally, there was a kicker to the scientists' finding on cheeseburgers.

"We certainly are not suggesting that people go out and chow down on cheese and hamburgers," one of the scientists said, adding that a balanced diet is best.

But he also said this: "People should be reassured to know there are things in food that *prevent* cancer."

I'm reassured, especially after the recent ordeal we've been through with apples and grapes.

In the time I have left here, I thought I might share some of my thoughts about cheeseburgers, given the fact I am quite the expert in this area.

1. Don't believe what I said earlier about it being hard to screw up a cheeseburger. Once, I ordered one in the airport in Zurich. The cheese was fine, but the burger tasted like a bowling shoe.

    It's probably not a good idea to order a cheeseburger in a foreign country unless you can find an American fast-food franchise.

    For the record, there is a McDonald's on the Champs Élysée in Paris. I've been there. Frankly, I enjoyed it more than I did Maxim's.

2. Never order a cheeseburger in a health-food restaurant. They might bring you a burger made out of soybeans. Soybean burgers would gag a rat.

3. For my money, the best fast-food cheeseburgers are at Wendy's, which makes up for their bad chili.

4. The very best cheeseburger is the one you cook at home. Buy fresh ground chuck, pound out a thick patty by hand, put it in a frying pan, and let it sit in its grease for as long as you can stand it. Eat it naked, so you don't run up a lot of dry-cleaning bills trying to get the grease stains out of your clothes.

5. The best cheeseburger bun is a plain one. Buns with seeds

on top or buns that come in any other shape besides round aren't fit for a cheeseburger. It says that in the Bible.
6. Anybody who doesn't like cheeseburgers is a communist. I went to Russia, and the only place I could find one was at the U.S. Embassy in Moscow. I rest my case.

Thank the Lord for the good news about cheeseburgers. I'm off to Wendy's to celebrate.

We Can't Stop Messing with Our Food

I actually saw a sign outside a health-food store in the trendy midtown section the other day advertising soybean ice cream.

I suppose, as a reporter, I should have gone inside and asked to see the soybean ice cream, but I was afraid they might want me to taste some, so I drove on.

Later, however, I began to think about soybean ice cream a little more deeply, and I came to two conclusions.

1. Yuk.
2. We're really starting to do some serious messing with our food.

Soybean ice cream, indeed. What is this? Some health-food junkie's idea of a joke?

There's nothing wrong with ice cream that I know of.

Eat enough of it, I suppose, and you'll outweigh the cow that gave the milk they used to make the ice cream, but if you can hold it down to a pint or two of Häagen-Dazs a week, and don't eat six Dove Bars at a single sitting, it's probably no big deal.

We can't leave food alone in this country. Either somebody is trying to force something down you that would gag a maggot just because it's good for you, or somebody is diddling around with what was perfect in the first place.

I was in a restaurant recently, and chicken noodle soup was on the menu. I like chicken noodle soup.

So I ordered it.

When the chicken noodle soup arrived, it didn't look anything like any chicken noodle soup I'd had before.

The noodles were too big.

"What sort of noodles are these?" I asked the waitress.

"Fettuccine," she answered.

"What did you do?" I asked. "Run out of regular chicken noodle soup noodles?"

"No," she answered. "Our chef is very creative."

That's the problem. People are getting too creative with our food and ruining it.

Whenever I am at a restaurant with which I am not familiar, I usually order a cheeseburger. It's hard to foul up anything as simple or inherently good as a cheeseburger.

Then I'm in this place and I order a cheeseburger and it comes to me with mushrooms on it.

"My God!" I scream when I see what has happened. "They've put mushrooms on my cheeseburger!"

"We always put mushrooms on our cheeseburgers," says my waiter, who has a ponytail and is wearing an earring. Never order a cheeseburger in a place where your waiter thinks he's Gidget.

Recently, I saw a commercial for fried chicken with a lot of hot spices in it. God never intended fried chicken to taste like some Mexican got loose in the batter with a pocketful of chili peppers.

I'm also baffled by cereal that comes from Europe and is

named after a mule. Don't forget to eat your Wheaties. You'll grow up to be like Michael Jordan, not a soccer player named Hans or Ivo.

Some order must return in this land of dancing, singing raisins, fast-food barbecue rib sandwiches, and Tommy Lasorda's "delicious milk shakes" that will make you lose weight. Lord help us, people are actually eating seaweed these days!

I don't want raw fish, anything remotely connected with soybeans, and mushrooms that taste like they sound, with the accent on the "mush."

Or, in the immortal words of my boyhood friend and idol, Weyman C. Wannamaker, Jr., a great American, when he tasted stewed prunes for the first and last time, "There's just some things that ain't fit to eat."

12 ME, MYSELF, AND I

The mating call of the Georgia Peach is
included in the following chapter. It got
The Donald, didn't it.

Legacy of the Love of Humor

The last of a special breed of folk is dead. There were twelve of them born to my paternal grandparents, Mama and Daddy Grizzard, of rural Gwinnett County, Georgia.

My father was the youngest. He's been gone twenty years. Aunt Nell was the oldest. She's been gone a long time, too.

Three of my late uncles were unforgettable characters. Walt and Wesley Grizzard were in the used-car business.

They had Grizzard Motors, and they were wily veterans of the trade. They were both big men with big voices, and very few customers escaped unsold when they stepped onto the lot.

"We're the walking man's best friend," my Uncle Wesley used to say.

My Uncle Frank was a lawyer. My father took me to see him perform in the courtroom once. I was maybe twelve.

Uncle Frank was defending a man on a charge of making moonshine.

As he addressed the jury, a woman seated behind the defendant broke into hysterical tears.

Uncle Frank went into his client's military history, pleading with the jury to realize he had "fought on the bald hills of Korea."

And the woman sobbed on.

It took ten minutes for the jury to render a verdict of Innocent.

As we walked out of the courtroom, my father said to Uncle Frank, "That sure was pitiful about the man's wife."

"Wife?" Uncle Frank asked back. "What wife?"

"Your client's wife," said my father. "It sure was pitiful the way she cried."

"That wasn't his wife," said Uncle Frank. "It was just an old girl I paid fifty dollars to come here and squall."

The last of the twelve was my Aunt Rufie. She died last week in suburban Atlanta. She was eighty-four.

She and my father were close. My parents divorced when I was six, and when I would visit my father in Atlanta, we would usually wind up at Aunt Rufie's house.

Daddy would play her piano and sing. I loved that house because of the laughter that was always in it.

When my father fell on hard times during the last years of his life, it was my Aunt Rufie who stood by him the strongest.

"I could never turn my back on my baby brother," she often said to me when we talked of him after his death.

I'm going to be a pallbearer at Aunt Rufie's funeral. I will see some cousins I haven't seen in years. Death brings survivors together, regardless of how far they might have drifted apart.

The Grizzard men and women, my uncles and aunts, meant a lot to me when I was a child. I lived with my mother and didn't see them that often, but when I did, it was always a grand experience.

The legacy they left me was the love of humor. There wasn't a one of them who couldn't brighten a room, and I'm still stealing a great deal of their material.

A man came up to me a few years ago at a public gathering and said, "I grew up with your dad and all his brothers and sisters. When folks got down in Gwinnett County, they'd send for a Grizzard just to cheer them up."

That's my heritage. I couldn't be prouder of it.

The Course of True Golf Never Runs Smooth

This is a true story. It took place about a year ago.

When I arrived home that evening, my mail was stacked on the counter at the kitchen stove.

A bill. A catalog or two advertising things I'd never buy. My *Sports Illustrated* had arrived. I ordered my subscription before you could get a sneaker phone with it. My timing has always been bad.

Then, there was the letter. It was addressed to me personally. In the left corner of the envelope were these words.

"Augusta National Golf Club."

Next, my eyes went to the postmark. "Augusta, Ga.," it said.

Why would the Augusta National Golf Club be writing me?

Had I applauded at the wrong time during one of my visits to the Club's Masters Golf tournament?

Had I referred to the Masters gallery as a "mob," which a network sportscaster once did and was never welcomed there after to cover the tournament?

With trembling hands I opened the envelope. The letter was on Augusta National stationery. It read:

"Dear Mr. Grizzard,

"Your name has come before the membership committee of the Augusta National Golf Club for consideration.

"I would like to invite you to a cocktail reception at the Club to meet you and discuss your possible invitation to become a member of the Club.

"As you must know, all matters of the Club must remain confidential.

"Please phone me as soon as possible to let me know if you'll be able to attend the reception May 15 at 7:30 P.M. at the Club."

The letter was signed by a person identifying himself as chairman of the Augusta National Membership Committee.

No way that the Augusta National Golf Club, the most prestigious in the country, was going to invite me to become a member.

I'd once heard they turned down Bob Hope. I was no captain of industry. Didn't they know my background?

Certainly I'm not embarrassed by my background—relatively poor rural white—but how many other members of the club had ever been in charge of taking out the slop bucket, the country version of the trash disposal?

But the letter did look official. And it was postmarked Augusta.

Then, my ego took over.

"Hey," I said to myself, "it's about time they invited me.

"I own a pair of Guccis. I've spent the night in a Ritz. I know to put the napkin in my lap the moment I sit down for dinner. I've got an eleven handicap. And I look good in green."

I got on the phone. I didn't care if it was after midnight.

Luckily, the first friend I awakened was in on it, and, upon hearing my excitement, decided I had taken the bait, which is what the joke was intended to do in the first place.

"It's a hoax," he admitted.

He named the other people involved and said they had made up some Augusta National stationery and then got somebody in Augusta to mail the letter to me.

"It was all in fun," he said.

I was more embarrassed than angry or disappointed.

"You dummy," I said to myself

Augusta National, indeed.

I had forgotten my place.

Georgia Peaches Can Be the Pits

The world is still reeling from the news that billionaire Donald Trump and his aging wife (she's forty-one, for Godsakes), Ivana, are nearing a split. Trouble, in other words, in Plazadise.

On top of that news has come another spicy tidbit inquiring minds also have been drooling over.

There is apparently another woman, and she is of all things, from Cohutta, Georgia (between Stinkrock and Roosterville), twenty-six-year-old model and part-time actress Marla Maples.

If the Trumps do get a divorce, Ivana is expected to walk with a total nearing the French war debt, or what a Colombian drug dealer can expect to bring home per month.

So can we expect in the future the possibility of Donald Trump taking up with Marla Maples full time? If he does, he will have latched on to one of the world's most intriguing characters, the Georgia Peach, bless her heart, and can I have a new Porsche, Daddy, the other one's dirty?

If Mr. T. thinks Ivana could go through a checkbook like grease through a goose, wait until he must deal with his cute little peachette, the former beauty queen, who, if she's like other GPs I have known, can go out in the morning with a credit card and come home at night with the writing worn slap off.

("Slap" is Georgia Peach for "completely.")

I married two Georgia Peaches myself. My third wife was from South Carolina. She was a lot more frugal than the other two. As she often said, "I never buy anything we don't really need."

"Do we really need this diamond-studded toilet seat?" I asked her the time she came home with a diamond toilet seat.

"It was on sale," she explained. "I saved you three hundred dollars."

I asked if I could have the three hundred I saved so I could buy a new set of tires for our car.

"There you go being careless with our money again," she said. "The tires are just as round as the day you bought them three years ago."

My two Georgia Peach ex-wives could shop with anybody. I took one to Greece. She tried to buy the Acropolis.

"Wouldn't it be cute in the backyard," she said.

I took another to Paris. I will never forget the concièrge at our hotel saying to my wife as she walked into the lobby after a shopping trip, "Madame Grizzard, would you like for me to store your packages? There's a vacant warehouse two blocks away."

Still, I must admit there is something very special about Georgia Peaches, like the good ones never perspire, they shave their legs everyday, and the sweetness they inherit from their mothers restrains the lion, e.g., D. T.

And if Donald Trump does wind up with Miss Maples, there're a few other things he should know about the little darlings:

- The mating call of the Georgia Peach: "Lordy, I'm sooooo drunk."
- The three men that the Georgia Peach admires most: 1. Daddy. 2. Daddy. 3. Daddy.
- What Georgia Peaches all have in common: They're always cold, and they have bladders the size of a white-acre pea.
- What two things you can always count on the Georgia Peach to know: what day the Dawgs play Clemson and the location of the nearest Neiman-Marcus.
- Why God made Georgia Peaches in the first place: to make up for the mistake he made on Joan Rivers.

More on this story as it becomes available, y'all.

Mama Goes Home

We buried Mom on her birthday, October 3. She would have been seventy-seven.

We were blessed with a beautiful autumn day. One of my mother's sisters remarked, "What if it had happened last week when we were having all that rain?"

We took Mama down to the little cemetery and put her next to her own mother. In the last year or so, Mama often would become confused and would ask relatives where her mother lived.

"She's dead, Christine," somebody would answer her.

She was Christine Causby Word Grizzard Atkinson, and she died from a disease called scleroderma. I don't know much about the disease except that doctors told us they had no way to cure it, and it killed my mother, slowly. It tortured her.

The family was trying to remember when Mama first got sick.

"It's been at least twenty years," was one thought.

But I knew to the day, almost. She was hospitalized for the first time on the day John Kennedy was buried. That was nearly twenty-six years ago. I watched the funeral on television in my mother's hospital room.

In the last years she spent all of her time in one of two places—either in a hospital bed in a hospital or in a hospital bed in the living room of her house.

I can't recall the last time I saw my mother standing.

She was a tiny thing in the end. I doubt she weighed a hundred pounds. And the painkillers never seemed to put her at ease for very long.

A preacher said to the family, "She's better off." He said it twice.

The mother who raised me had been gone for a long time already. That happens so often. The parent becomes the child and the child, the parent.

And, yes, her suffering, as far as we know, is over.

But it still hurts when I think I will never see her again. Will never hear her speak. Will never get to lean over her in that bed and stroke her hair and kiss her and say, "Mama, I love you," and hear her strained reply, "And I love you, too, sugar."

What she had to go through in her life. I wrote a eulogy that was read at her funeral, and I said, "It seemed that every time something good happened to my mother, something bad inevitably followed."

She fell in love with my father and a child was born. But she had to send her husband off to war, twice. And war destroyed him and took him away from her.

After a time she did find another man's love. They were married thirty-five years, but for twenty-five of those years, she was so ill she could not enjoy the good parts about being a wife.

Her legacy, though, is she never went quietly. After my father was gone, she was faced with finding a way to provide for herself and her child. She was already in her forties at a time women had no easy access to financial security of their own.

But she worked by day and went to school at night, and if there were a Hall of Fame for first-grade teachers, she would be in it.

And the illness. Her doctor said, "I've never seen a patient fight for her life as hard as she has."

Ten years ago the doctors were telling us to prepare for the end. *Ten years ago.*

My mother loved me. She protected me. She praised me. She consoled me. She gave me knowledge and values. She inspired me. And when there was no man available, she went outside and tossed a baseball with me.

I should have called her more often.

Good-bye to Mr. Bob

I was back in my hometown church for the second time in only a few months.

In October, I was there for my mother's funeral. And such a short time later I was back for the funeral of a man who I used to wish was my father.

I didn't have a father growing up. A divorce took care of that.

But I did have Bob Entrekin. Bobby, his son, and I went to school together from the second grade through college. He was in my first wedding. I was in his only wedding.

I called Bobby's dad "Mr. Bob." Years later, when I was grown, I was still calling him "Mr. Bob."

"You can drop that 'mister,'" he said.

I couldn't have dropped it if I had tried—which I had no intention of doing. Respect should have no time limits.

When I was a child, the other kids had daddies. Since I didn't, I adopted Mr. Bob. I didn't know much about the term then, but now I do.

Mr. Bob had class. Loads of it. I suppose that was what drew me to him.

Mr. Bob taught himself class. He grew up hard with no chance to go to college. But he read. He read about history, about art, about music.

He had two special heroes, Churchill and Beethoven. I spent a lot of Saturday nights at Mr. Bob's house: He and his son and I tuned to a night college football game on the radio. Mr. Bob was a good Georgia Bulldog.

And Sunday morning we always would awaken to the unlikely sounds of Beethoven filling Mr. Bob's tiny frame house.

"Boys," he would say to Bobby and me as we prepared for Sunday School, "this is what good music is all about."

Mr. Bob was an immaculate dresser. He had a firm, bounding voice. He and his wife, Miss Willie, often traveled abroad.

He could speak about any subject. What class I have—and some agree it is very little—I learned from Mr. Bob Entrekin.

The cancer that eventually killed him forced Mr. Bob into early retirement as rural mail carrier.

At the funeral, the preacher, the same who was a comfort at my mother's service, said, "Every child in town knew exactly what time Bob would arrive at their house. He always had a piece of candy for them."

The entire community loved him. When he died, the old cried with the young.

The preacher also offered a favorite Churchill quote of Mr. Bob's. A pretty young woman stood and sang "Amazing Grace." When they rolled Mr. Bob's casket, covered with a flag, out of the packed little church, the organist played a Beethoven piece.

He was quite a man, a self-educated man of so many interests, a man who taught himself to appreciate extraordinary beauty and accomplishment.

And it was beauty and examples of brilliant endeavor that were his proof of the existence of his God.

Mr. Bob Entrekin made a difference in my life, and a month before he died, I told him so.

Daddies need to hear that sort of thing from their sons.

If Hank Gathers Had Only Listened to His Heart

A lot of people who watched that awful tape that showed Hank Gathers convulsing and dying on the basketball floor probably asked, "Why did he keep playing? He knew he had a heart problem."

I know why he did it. He did it because he was twenty-three years old, basketball was his life and his planet, and he was certain he would live forever—heart problem or no heart problem.

I've been there. When I was fifteen, I had to have a physical in order to play in a baseball tournament. The doctor listened to my heart and told my mother and me that I had a "heart murmur."

The first thing I asked the doctor was, "Can I still play ball?"

He said I could, but to keep my heart checked regularly. If he had said I couldn't play, I probably would have found a way to play anyway.

I basically forgot about my heart murmur. I played baseball and basketball in high school. It never occurred to me I could drop dead in the middle of the game.

I lived for sports, and I was certain I would live forever, too.

I took up tennis when I was twenty-three. I played tennis every day.

When I was thirty-five, my doctor called me into his office after a physical and told me my heart murmur was actually a faulty aortic valve.

Then, he said the most frightening words I've ever heard in my life.

"You need heart surgery."

My first question, even at thirty-five? Simple:

"Can I still play tennis after this is over?"

The doctor said, "We'll see."

The operation was a success. My doctor said I could play tennis again as long as I stuck to doubles and didn't get overtired.

I played singles and continued to play every day. Often I played all day long.

Three years later, I had a second valve surgery. The first implant became infected and had to be replaced. I came close to dying.

But even after that, the doctors still said I could play tennis under the previous restrictions, which I had ignored.

But I wasn't fifteen, or even thirty-five anymore. I was over forty.

I tried playing tennis again, but a new thought had crept inside my head. That thought was: Is it safe for me to be running around out here on the tennis court with heart disease?

I decided I could drop dead on the court. I gave up tennis.

If Hank Gathers had lived long enough, that question eventually would have gotten to him.

He might even have quit pro basketball in the midst of his prime.

Aging does things like that. It puts you eyeball to eyeball with reality.

I must have seen that tape ten times on television, and each time I saw it, I thought, That could have happened to me.

This heart thing will kill me one day, if something else doesn't get me first.

But I'm thankful I at least got twenty more years than Hank Gathers got.

And every new day is a bonus.

Love and Hate
Mail Call

People ask, "Do you read all your mail?"

Of course I do. The mail is great fun.

I get letters that say I'm a terrific guy. I get letters that say I'm a disgrace.

I enjoy both kinds. The love mail fires my ego and makes me feel wanted.

The hate mail tells me I'm hitting nerves and stirring things up. I've always been an irreverent little cuss.

The hate mail is also enjoyable because of the names I get called. Here are some examples I've collected over the years:

- "You Godless Gizzard."
- "You Tunnel-Visioned Toad."
- "You Ignorant Maggot."
- "You Four-eyed, Fur-mouthed, Fish-faced fool."

These come from religious nuts, gun lovers, bleeding-heart liberals, soccer fans, and the left-handed Chinese Yacht Racers Anti-Defamation League.

But the all-time all-time came in the other day.

A man who signed himself as A.M. Lamar of Montgomery, Ala., put me in my place as no one ever has before.

Mr. Lamar took exception to a column I wrote suggesting we immediately kick butt in Iraq, which sounded like a good idea at the time.

His letter began: "Like most childless, middle-aged, medically deferred megamouths, you just can't wait to see someone else's young sons charge in to "kick butt' in another bloody and stupid patriotic war."

Brilliant. In one sentence, Mr. Lamar refers to my inability to stay married, my advancement to middle age (a sure sign of stupidity), my health problems, and my occasional tendency toward mindless pontification.

But that wasn't the best part. Here's what Mr. Lamar's letter said next:

"Are you ready to volunteer in Iraq, you pecksniffian, pusillanimous, pig-valved (rhymes with 'hiss') ant?"

That is taking alliteration to previously uncharted heights.

"Pusillanimous" you can look up. It's "lacking courage of spirit; cowardly."

And I do have an aortic valve that once belonged to a pig, and you certainly should know of the lowly ant to which Mr. Lamar refers and how it implies that one is terribly insignificant, as in "run you little (rhymes with 'hiss') ants" (from the movie *The Last Picture Show*).

"Pecksniffian" took some work. I went to the *Random House Dictionary of the English Language*, second edition, unabridged, and there it was.

It comes from the Seth Pecksniff character in *Martin Chuzzlewit*, a novel by Dickens.

Pecksniffian's definition read, "Hypocritically and unctuously affecting benevolence or high moral principles"—whatever that means.

So I went to "unctuous." It is, "characterized by excessive piousness."

Basically, I think "pecksniffian" means I'm an ignorant maggot.

At any rate I wanted A.M. Lamar to know how much I appreciate his letter and that his points were well taken and I'm also glad "pecksniffian" didn't mean anything dirty.

They Wag Their Tails, Not Their Tongues

The New York Times Sunday Magazine has done an article on me. There must not have been much news around fit to print.

I will not comment otherwise on the article, but I would like to say a few words about a quotation that appeared from the ex–Mrs. Grizzard Kathy Schmook, aka Number 3.

Mrs. Schmook, who lives in Montana, is quoted as saying, "Lewis is the loneliest man in the world."

It was a nice gesture, I thought, that my local paper pulled out the quote and ran it so that readers of these papers, or at least those who read them, were able to see it, too.

I wonder if my ex-wife had said, "Lewis is the greatest lover in the world," or, "Lewis always wears clean underwear," if that would have made *The New York Times Sunday Magazine*, and my local paper as well, but she didn't, so we can go on.

I don't know why Mrs. Schmook said that. We haven't talked in years.

But I would like to say to her, *The New York Times*, and just for the everlasting record that, although like most people, I do go through periods of loneliness, I am not the loneliest man in the world.

I figure Manuel Noriega is the loneliest man in the world. Either him or Mikhail Gorbachev or Pete Rose.

I'm probably not even the loneliest man or person on my street. If for no other reason it's because I've got my two dogs, Catfish and Cornbread, the black Labs.

Catfish and Cornbread love me. They begin each night asleep on their L. L. Bean doggie beds.

Catfish's bed is at the foot of mine. Cornbread's is to the right. At some point in the middle of every night, however, Cornbread, my youngest, gets out of his bed and gets into mine.

Each morning I awaken with Cornbread next to me.

At first, I tried to discourage this. But then I thought, it's comforting to know that at least somebody or something wants to sleep next to me at night no matter what I did during the day.

Dogs are like that. They are forgiving and completely non-judgmental.

When I come home, Catfish and Cornbread are always glad to see me. They care not where I have been, what I have been doing, or with whom I have been doing it.

I can tell that is true by the way Cornbread leaps at my feet first and attempts to lick me on the head.

I can tell that by the way Catfish whines, wags his tail, and seems to be saying, "Am I glad you're home! Want to go in the backyard and throw me some tennis balls?"

I sort of wish Catfish and Cornbread could read. They would glance at *The New York Times Sunday Magazine* and say, "Whoa, listen to this: 'Lewis is the loneliest man in the world.' Hey, Dad, if you're lonely, we know a Dalmation and two basset hounds up the street we could ask over and have a party."

I'm not lonely. Sometimes, I don't sleep that well at night, onions give me heartburn, I'm upset about what's happening in Khartoum, but I'm not lonely, because my dogs love me and don't mouth off to newspapers.

Now, if you'll excuse me, I'm late for Cornbread's Little League game.

One Man's Fill of Pills

Because of a continuing problem with a leaking, artificial aortic valve in my heart, my doctor has given me a lot of pills to take.

I've never been much of one to take pills. In fact, I've always hated to take pills.

I've got one of those throats that, when confronted with a pill, screams, "Pill!" and tries to gag me. I've always hated gagging, too.

It's been hell taking all the pills my doctor has prescribed. Here is my daily pill agenda:

- Blue Ones: three times a day.
- Yellow Ones: same.
- Big White One: one a day.
- Little White ones: four a day.
- Big, Nasty-Looking Slick Red One: once a day, with food.
- Green Ones: six at bedtime.

It is amazing how having to take all those pills has changed my life.

I suddenly have to be a lot more responsible.

Before, all I really had to be responsible about was writing my column, feeding my dogs, feeding myself, wearing my seat belt, and keeping my head down when I strike at a golf ball.

Now, I've got to be responsible for all that, plus taking my pills.

I take my first batch first thing in the morning. Gagging for fifteen minutes is a great way to start a new day.

Then, when I go out, I have to remember to put my noon pills in my pocket. Put a lot of pills in your pocket for a few hours and they will get all sorts of stuff on them like pocket lint, which probably has a lot of germs on it since nobody really knows what pocket lint is. What if it's like asbestos or contains radon gas?

Occasionally, some of my pocket pills fall out of my pocket and I'll be caught away from home without them. What would Karl Malden do in that situation?

Should I dash home for replacements? Can I wait until I get home in the evening and then take two?

Has anybody put any cyanide in my pills? Are there any rodent hairs in them like Ralph Nader says you can find in hot dogs? Can I do the Heimlich maneuver on myself if I get choked on one of these pills? Can you die from gagging?

All these pills may be good for my heart, but what about the effect they are having on my nerves?

When I do manage to sleep, I have nightmares about being attacked by thousands of Carter's Little Liver Pills that have faces that look like my pharmacist, a former oil-tanker captain.

I see an aspirin commercial on television and I get a migraine. One other nightmare: I dream I have to take all my pills and all I have to take them with is a glass of warm buttermilk.

We take so many pills in this country, there must be some pills for pill stress.

I'd ask my doctor for some, but I'm afraid he would give them to me.

Touching Memories
of Touch Football

Danny Thompson was my first best friend. We met in second grade.

Danny was the fastest boy in class and was always picked first when we chose sides for touch football.

I used to practice running alone at home thinking I would learn something that would magically transform me into what the sports pages used to refer to as a "speed merchant."

Nothing worked. Danny and I are both forty-four now, and we haven't raced in more than thirty years, but I know I still couldn't outrun him. It is a reality I have accepted.

A dear friend threw me a birthday party at her home last week. It was more like a class reunion.

"How did we all get this old this fast?" we asked each other.

Danny was there. We started telling the old stories again, and I told the same ones I always tell on him.

It's the story about his damned football. I might have accepted the fact I will never be able to outrun Danny Thompson, but I hadn't gotten over the football.

We played touch football on Sunday afternoons in a vacant lot.

We started playing with Bobby Entrekin's football, but it didn't age very well. So my mother bought me one, and I threw it into the Sunday games.

But it was showing the signs of wear, too, a couple of years later when Christmas came and we were all twelve.

But no problem. Danny's dad gave him a new football for

Christmas. He showed it to me Christmas afternoon in his house.

"Nice ball," I said to Danny. "Let's go outside and play pass."

"Not with my ball," he said.

"Why not?"

"I don't want to get it dirty," he answered, and put the ball back in its box.

We never used Danny's football. Never. Sunday afternoon games broke up when we graduated from high school, and as far as I know, Danny's ball was still in its box.

"So what ever happened to that damned football of yours?" I asked him at the party.

"I guess Daddy threw it away when I went into service," he said, and we had the same good laugh at this story we always do.

Later, Danny handed me a present. "It's something you've wanted for a long time," he said.

I ripped off the paper and opened the box. It was a new football. Not THE original football of thirty years ago, but it was in fact a new football.

"Now, will you quit complaining about my football?" Danny laughed.

I put my arms around him and thanked him.

He's forgiven.

The county built a fire station on our old football field. But we said maybe before too much longer we'd all get together again for an old-timers' game of touch.

"I'll bring the ball," I said, "if I can choose first when we pick sides."

I'd still pick Danny.

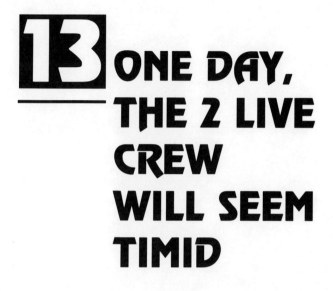

13 ONE DAY, THE 2 LIVE CREW WILL SEEM TIMID

I said earlier in the introduction what I think about rap. Here, I discuss the Milli Vanilli controversy. I vote they change their name to Tutti-Frutti.

Justify My
Madonna

I was about half-asleep Monday night when *Nightline* came on my bedroom television.

Forrest Sawyer, sitting in for Ted Koppel, who was having his hair done, announced that Madonna—probably the best female singer who regularly appears on-stage in her underclothes—would be his guest.

I opened my other eye.

Normally, I would prefer a *Nightline* interview with a Middle Eastern diplomat with an unpronounceable name, but I admit I had been intrigued by a recent development regarding Madonna, who, speaking of development, has done a rather good job of it.

I prefer Reba McEntire when it comes to female vocalizing, but Madonna is out with a hot new music video that has the entertainment world in a fitful stir at the moment.

The video, *Justify My Love*, was recently turned down by the network that plays music videos, MTV.

I'm not a big fan of MTV, either, but often as I am flicking down my cable menu searching for a *Mr. Ed* rerun, or a World War II documentary, I come across MTV.

On these occasions I see things that amaze me. I see people in various stages of undress, dancing and cavorting in such suggestive ways my glasses fog up and my fingers are rendered unable to press the channel button to get this sort of thing out of my view.

My doctor revealed to me I was suffering from MTV paralysis, a condition that often strikes adults when they see things on television they wouldn't expect to see in a darkened, X-rated movie theater with a lotta guys sitting around in raincoats.

Thus, my intrigue. If MTV won't show Madonna's new video, then the video is something I absolutely must see.

And *Nightline*, which didn't have anybody left to ask whether the economic sanctions in Iraq were working, showed it.

I will attempt to describe what I saw on the video the best I can.

The video was in black-and-white; I'm sure about that. But I can't tell you exactly who was doing what to whom and how often.

There were simply too many individuals involved—and I use the term individuals here because it wasn't easy to pick out genders, either.

I do know that Madonna, the scantily clad, pouting seductress, and the guy who looked like Sal Mineo wearing a pencil-thin mustache were obviously more than just friends.

Once again my glasses fogged up, and when I tried to switch the channel off what I determined to be an orgy set to music, my hand was once again rendered in a complete state of paralysis.

So, I watched the entire thing.

Do I think MTV was right not to show such an explicit video?

While I did note there were no barnyard animals or hand-held power tools shown in the video, indicating there were some tasteful limitations put on its production, I'm glad to see MTV will at least draw the line somewhere.

Do I think the fact that the video will not be shown on MTV will cause it to suffer financially?

Absolutely not. Anything that steamy and controversial will be bought up by every kid in the country.

After seeing Madonna romp around in the aforementioned sexual smorgasbord, do I still think she is less talented than Reba McEntire?

Who is Reba McEntire?

Del Shannon Was a Runaway Hit

They found Del Shannon at his California home with a bullet in his head, and they called it suicide. He was only fifty-five.

I'm fully aware at this point there may be those responding to that opening paragraph by asking, "Who on earth was Del Shannon?"

I'll tell you. He was a fifties and sixties rock and roll star. Rock and roll stars from that era were different from those of today.

They didn't appear on stage half-naked, they didn't smash their guitars, they didn't bite the heads off chickens or bats, and, for the most part, you could understand the words they were singing and their music was no threat to any of your ear parts.

And one of those aforementioned exceptions involve Del Shannon. His biggest hit was titled "Runaway," a classic you still can hear on those oldies radio stations.

I've been listening to "Runaway" since it was recorded in 1961 and had never been able to understand a couple of words of the chorus:

"I'm a-walkin' in the rain/*something, something* and I feel the pain."

I was talking to my friend Carol Dunn, a fifties and sixties rock and roll expert.

She said, "That was terrible about Del Shannon. I saw him perform a couple of years ago. He seemed so alive onstage. I wonder what would make him kill himself."

Suicide is always a puzzle.

I asked Carol Dunn if she knew all the words to "Runaway."
She said she did. I said, "What comes after "I'm a-walkin' in the
rain . . . ?"

She sang it.

"I'm a-walkin in the rain/*teardrops fall* and I feel the pain."

I felt like a huge burden had been lifted off my shoulders.

After all these years, I finally knew the missing words to the
"Runaway" chorus.

We talked some more.

"Look how many of those old stars are gone," I said. "Elvis, of
course, and Roy Orbison and Bill Haley."

"And James Brown's in jail," said Carol.

We surmised that this meant we were getting older. When the
musicians who played the background music while you grew up
begin to die, it's obviously a sign of rampant aging like swollen
joints in your fingers and not understanding MTV.

I did notice this, however: Del Shannon's obituary made *Time*
magazine, an obvious indication that a lot of people think the life
he took from himself was a significant one, even if he didn't think
so.

It was a great song, "Runaway." Thanks, Del.

Willy-Nilly
Milli Vanilli

There was a photograph in the papers the other day of Milli Vanilli, the rock duo that won Best New Artist Grammys for their best-selling single and album, *Girl You Know It's True*.

Now, they're singing the blues, since it was all a fraud. Milli Vanilli were moving their lips and Milli Vanilli were making a few million smackers, but somebody else, whose name escapes me, was doing the singing.

I studied the photograph at length. Sideways, too. The question occurred to me, which of these birds was Milli and which was Vanilli?

They both had long hair and soft features—a nice way of saying either could pass for a girlperson in a dimly lit room.

But I decided the one on the left was Vanilli and the one on the right was the other one.

Milli sort of reminded me of a pagan dancer in one of those old biblical movies. That and a fortune-teller named Madame Ruth I once visited to see if there would be anything left of my fortune after the divorce trial.

This is not to say I didn't also have some doubts as to just how high Vanilli's testosterone level goes, but if I had to go out with one of them or die, I'd pick Milli and go someplace very crowded. Like Istanbul, where I don't know a soul.

To be perfectly honest about it, the fact that Milli Vanilli's music-making was a hoax (which would be an even better word were it pronounced ho-axe) doesn't bother me at all.

First, before the news about the chicanery broke, I had never heard of Milli Vanilli.

Asked to identify Milli Vanilli at a previous time, I would have been like most middle-aged individuals—who think all music made since 1962 is the work of bed-wetting subversives—and guessed, the Italian version of Hägen-Dazs?

Second, I like an occasional ho-axe, and if the truth be known, the public likely has been hoodwinked in this manner lots of times.

What if:

- Johnny Carson isn't really that funny and Ed McMahon is a master ventriloquist?
- The 2 Live Crew are actually Bible-thumping, polite, nerdy intellectuals who want to reveal their true selves, but their agent won't let them, fearing drops in album sales?
- *Rocky V* is *Rocky II* played backward?
- Wrestling isn't really fake? It's just a bunch of loud no-necks who don't know how to fight very well?
- Jesse Helms is gay?
- *Saturday Night Live* is taped Thursday morning?
- Saddam Hussein is actually a pussycat?
- The Bush administration was behind the whole Milli Vanilli thing in an effort to shift focus to somebody else whose lips got them into serious trouble?

Think about it. The president's dog is also named Millie (the "e" is silent), and the more I looked at Vanilli, the more convinced I became he actually could be Dan Quayle disguised as a tribal warrior with a serious hormone imbalance.

And didn't Watergate start sort of the same way? Stay tuned. This could get interesting.

The Filth They Call Music

A man who said he had two teenaged daughters wrote and asked if I would comment on, as he put it, "the filth they're selling as music these days."

So happy to oblige, and I must agree with the man that the filth they are selling as music these days isn't really music, just a guy with a deep voice saying a lot of dirty words while somebody beats on a barrel with a two-iron and somebody else kills a cat in the background.

Music music at least should have a tune so you can hum it while you kill a cat.

Also, the man who wrote isn't the only person who is concerned about the filth they are selling as music these days.

The governor of Florida is concerned, for instance. He wants the state's prosecutor to find a way to keep a recording by something called The 2 Live Crew away from minors.

I saw a photograph of The 2 Live Crew in the paper. They were four young men who looked more like somebody's starting backfield than a recording group, but what do I know?

Bette Midler looks more like a linebacker than a singer, but she did a pretty good job on "Wind Beneath My Wings."

The 2 Live Crew has a blockbuster hit out titled, "Me So Horny." I have never heard the recording, but *The Washington Post* called it "A misogynist's catalog of aggressive sexual acts, delivered in lewd and lurid detail."

Translated, that means the lyrics are so filthy you would be appalled if you heard them, thus making your teenaged daughters drool for the first opportunity to get their hot little ears on them, too.

What I think is people like the governor of Florida and the man who wrote me are wasting their time.

That's because there is an ageless equation that goes, "Nothing sells like controversy."

There's this guy in New York named Bernie, see. He works for a record label. He wears a toupee and a jewelry store around his neck.

When The 2 Live Crew first brought their recording to him, it was titled, "The Wind in Your Hair."

But Bernie's smart. He said to The 2 Live Crew, "That won't sell eight copies. Call it "Me So Horny' and make it filthy and get back to me in thirty minutes."

So, The 2 Live Crew puts out a misogynist's catalog of aggressive sexual acts, delivered in lewd and lurid detail, parents get upset, the governor of Florida gets upset, and kids flock to record stores to buy it, and Bernie gets rich and the recording group gets rich.

Legislation won't stop the aforementioned equation from working. All that will stop it is to ignore The 2 Live Crew and "Me So Horny," thus taking away the thrill your kids get when they listen to such.

That way, your children will go back to dyeing their hair orange, or whatever else they can think of to drive you crazy, and The 2 Live Crew will sign with Clemson, and Bernie will have to find a real job.

Like being a pimp.

One Day, The 2 Live Crew Will Seem Timid

They will laugh at us twenty years from now for all the stir and commotion The 2 Live Crew, the rap rascals with the dirty mouths, have caused.

Sure they will.

We look back and laugh at our parents and our teachers and our lawmakers and our ministers for how they reacted to Elvis, don't we?

Remember that? All Elvis did was shake his pelvis.

He did a little grind with his hips, is what he did, and you would have thought he had uncovered his privates onstage, which is what one of today's rock stars did not long ago.

With every Elvis move, the teenage girls screamed with delight, and the adults decried the Sideburned One as vile and evil.

"It's the devil's music," I heard the Baptist preacher back home say.

"Listen to that music," he continued, "and you are on a path headed straight to hell!"

I was ten or eleven at the time, and I certainly didn't want to get on the freeway to hell—and I still don't—but I took a chance.

I went home after church, took out my 45 of "Don't Be Cruel," listened to it a couple of times, and then prayed, "Don't hold it against me, Lord, I just like the beat."

There are people now who want The 2 Live Crew's concerts and records banned.

When I was growing up, the old men called Elvis's offerings "jungle music," and then said worse about him.

But we look back on Elvis now, and if he were still alive, we could invite him to sing in church. They play his music on country-music stations, for crying out loud. Fifty-year-old women visit his grave and cry.

Eventually, the same thing will happen to The 2 Live Crew. Today they get arrested and the cops monitor their concerts.

And that just makes the kids even more anxious to buy the group's music and see them perform.

They flock to the record stores, and they think the dirty lyrics are a hoot, as we did when we heard the unintelligible words to "Louie, Louie" were really filthy if you could hear them. And the kids flock to see The 2 Live Crew perform, and although I think The 2 Live Crew and their music—if you can call it that—are enough to make you puke, if I were sixteen, I wouldn't miss a performance.

We've gone from Elvis to The 2 Live Crew in my lifetime. Twenty years from now The 2 Live Crew will, like Elvis, seem absolutely harmless.

God knows what they'll be doing twenty years from now. Singing onstage in the nude, probably. Madonna sings in her underwear now.

They'll be singing naked and probably having sex onstage, and the kids who liked The 2 Live Crew will have their drawers in a serious bundle because their kids will be determined to hear and see Stark Nakkid and the Car Thieves singing their controversial hit, "I Want to Kiss You on Your Woo-Woo in the Nude."

The point is, you ain't seen nothin' yet. Elvis seems like an angel now, and a generation from now, The 2 Live Crew probably won't be able to get a gig playing a Tupperware party. So, nobody have a cow over The 2 Live Crew. This, too, will pass for something even more shocking.

It always does.

14 OBNOXIOUS PEOPLE IN THE NEWS

The War in the Gulf certainly was not another Vietnam. Jane Fonda, who's been hanging out with Ted Turner, didn't go to Baghdad. And Nixon lies to us again.

Trumped-up Tale

Donald Trump's chief accountant, Fillmore, sat down in The Donald's plush office.

"What is it this time, Filbert?" asked The Donald.

"It's Fillmore," said the accountant.

"Details. What do you need to see me about?"

"I have some bad news for you, sir."

"What is it, Philpot?"

"We're out of cash, sir."

"What do you mean, 'We're out of cash, sir'?"

"I mean just what I said—we don't have any money."

"Well, you idiot, call the bank and arrange for them to send some over."

"I've already tried that, Mr. Trump. The bank won't loan us any more money until we've paid back what we already owe them."

"Pay them back, Fennimore?"

"Yes, sir. That's how banks make their money. They loan money to you, and then you pay it back with interest."

"I always wondered how that worked. Well, there's another solution. Sell off some real estate."

"I'm afraid that's impossible, sir. The real estate market is very soft, and there's the matter of your pending divorce. The court would likely stop us from selling off anything until your settlement with Mrs. Trump is completed."

"What else could we do?"

"May I be perfectly frank, sir?"

"You can be anything you want to be as long as you know the art of the deal."

"What I mean, sir, is, can I be completely truthful?"

"Certainly, Frank."

"There's nothing you can do. You're finished. You're tapped out. It's Negative Cash Flow City."

"But how could this happen?"

"It was your extravagance and greed, sir."

"Extravagance and greed?"

"Like the time you spent—and I have the exact figures here with me—$17,478.66 to fly to Rio with Miss Maples for dinner."

"That much? But we didn't even have dessert. Okay, so that's a little extravagant but I've never been greedy."

"I beg to differ, Mr. Trump. Remember when you tried to buy New Hampshire?"

"But I've always wanted my own New England state since I was a little boy."

"Yes, and if the deal had come through, you were going to make everybody in New Hampshire move to Iowa so you would have some privacy."

"I forget why that deal didn't come through."

"You decided to spend the money on your hotel and casino in Atlantic City."

"How's that doing, Finneman?"

"Snake eyes."

"No matter, Finkelstein, I've still got a good woman to stand by my side during the hard times."

"Not anymore, sir."

"You mean Marla has . . . ?"

"Her exact words were, 'I don't do ex-billionaires.' But there is some good news, sir."

"What is it, Phinezy?"

"There is a concerted effort in this country to do something about the homeless. I'm certain they'll have shelter for you within the month."

"I'm a street person?"

"You start in the morning at eight. Good-bye, Mr. Frump."

Jim Bakker: A Man with Convictions

The Lewis Grizzard Fantasy Column. Fantasies about obnoxious people in the news:

Clunk!

The cell door slams shut.

"Well, hi there, my name is Jim Bakker, and I'm your new roommate—I mean, cellmate."

No response.

"Maybe you didn't hear me, I said, 'Well, hi there, my name is Jim Bakker, and I'm your new cellmate.' "

"They call me Mad Dog."

"What an interesting name. Why do they call you that?"

"Because I bite the heads off cats."

"Very interesting. Is that why you're in prison?"

"You writin' a book?"

"No. It's just that if we're going to have to share this small space for the next forty-five years, I thought it might be nice if we knew something about each other."

"What you in for?"

"They say I defrauded some people out of some money."

"You're a thief."

"Well, not in the strictest sense. You see, I was a televangelist and . . ."

"A what?"

"A televangelist. I preached on television, and people sent me a lot of money to help me with the Lord's work."

"Like I said, you're a thief."

"Wait a minute, Mad Dog. It was just that my wife has expensive tastes and you take a few million here and a few million there and, pretty soon, you're talking about a lot of money."

"Last cellmate I had was a thief. I hate thieves."

"And what happened to your last cellmate?"

"I bit his head off."

"I see. Well, do you want me to take the upper bunk or the lower?"

"Lower's mine."

"Fine, then I'll take the upper."

"Upper's mine, too."

"Okay. Then I just get over here in the corner in the fetal position. I hope you don't mind some light whimpering."

"You got a funny face."

"I beg your pardon."

"I said, 'You got a funny face.' My brother had a funny face."

"What a coincidence. And what happened to your brother?"

"I bit his head off. He looked like a cat. You look like a cat, too."

"Mad Dog, please. We're going to be in this cell together for a long time, and we're simply not getting off on the right foot. I think it's important that we develop some sort of relationship."

"You gettin' fresh with me?"

"Of course not."

"Had another cellmate got fresh one time."

"Let me guess. You bit his head off."

"No. I cut his throat in the exercise yard."

"Well, I can assure you I won't attempt to get fresh with you."

"Why not? Don't like my looks?"

"It's not that, Mad Dog. It's just that I don't want to offend you in anyway."

"You think I'm ugly, don't you?"

"I never said that, Mad Dog. You're quite attractive. As a matter of fact, you remind me a lot of my wife."

"You sayin' I look like a woman?"

"No. I'm saying my wife has hair all over her back, too."

"Hand me that box over there, preacher man."

"What's in it?"

"My mascara."

Next in the Lewis Grizzard Fantasy Column: Zsa Zsa slaps Mike Tyson and takes a trip to outer space.

Nixon Caught in Another Lie

I finally got around to reading the excerpts from Richard Nixon's latest book, *In the Arena*, which appeared a couple of weeks ago in *Time*.

According to *Time*, the book is "an emotional and extraordinarily candid memoir."

I would call it "whiny."

Nixon writes of ". . . The myths of Watergate, the smoke screen of false charges that ultimately undercut my administration's ability to govern effectively."

Any credibility I might have sensed in such statements were dashed when Tricky Dicky decided to write about his golf game. Get this:

"I quit golf 10 years ago, though I enjoyed the game. One day, in late 1979, I broke 80.

"It was on a relatively easy course in San Clemente, but for me it was like climbing Mount Everest. I knew I could never get better, so the competitive challenge was gone. . . ."

Hold it. Hold it. Hold it.

Richard Milhous Nixon broke 80? The same man who triple-bogeyed the presidency?

Do you know how difficult it is for even a fairly competent golfer to break 80? On even the easiest of golf courses?

Damn hard. And Richard Nixon, then in his sixties, broke that incredibly tough barrier?

Who was keeping score? Liddy?

There's a photograph of Nixon swinging a golf club included in the excerpt. Get out of here!

His pants practically come up to his neck, and he looks more like a man trying to hit a snake with a tree limb than somebody belting one 250 down the middle, which is what you have to do quite consistently if you can break 80.

How did Dick Nixon break 80? Did his scores on five holes mysteriously disappear?

Were Haldeman, Ehrlichman, and Mitchell the witnesses?

If you can't trust Richard Nixon to run the presidency, how can you trust him on a golf course?

He'd move his ball in the rough when you weren't looking. Of course he would. He'd lie about what he had on a hole.

"What did you make there, Mr. President?" Liddy would ask.

"Par, Gordon," Nixon would answer.

Sure. After he took a mulligan on his drive that went out of bounds, tossed his second shot out of the sand trap by hand, and said he took two putts instead of the three he actually took, Liddy—ever the company man—wrote down "four."

Go eat a rat, Gordon. I don't believe Richard Nixon when he

says he broke 80 in golf. I think he's lying to us again, like he did on TV.

"The myths of Watergate," indeed. The myths of Richard Nixon's golf game.

Would you buy a used car from this man? Would you believe him when he says he's found his ball after hitting it into the deep woods? Would you believe him if he had the pencil and says you lost two ways on the back nine and owe him ten bucks?

You would? My handicap is 36. Call me. We'll play.

You're Hanoi-ing Me, Jane

Jane Fonda is what's wrong with the Atlanta Braves.

Ted Turner, who owns the Braves, is too busy messing with that exercise freak to notice his baseball team is still as lousy as ever and may set a record for not drawing flies to the ballpark.

I'm not certain how Ted Turner got mixed up with Hanoi Jane in the first place. Who introduced them? Ho Chi Minh? No, he's dead. Maybe it was former California governor Jerry Brown.

I never trusted Governor Moonbeam, either.

Ted, the Braves have no bullpen, no hitting, and they only drew eleven thousand to the home opener, and half of them probably saw the lights on at the stadium and thought there was a tractor pull going on.

Instead of hanging out with Jane at the Academy Awards bash, you should have been back home trying to figure out how to unload Andres Thomas for a relief pitcher.

You can already see some of the effects Miss Fonda is having on Captain Outrageous.

Ted recently banned the F-word at his place of business.

If you work for Ted Turner, you can't say "foreign" anymore. You've got to say, "international."

That sounds like something a bleeding-heart liberal left of Michael Dukakis would be behind.

What's wrong with the word "foreign"?

—"*Foreign* investors buy Iowa."

—"My wife left me, my kids hate me, the factory closed because it can't compete with *foreign* manufacturers and my dog got run over by an Isuzu. I think I'll join the *Foreign* Legion."

Does Ted Turner have an airplane? I'm sure he does. What does it say in the rest room?

"Do not flush any *international* objects down the toilet?"

What can we expect next, Ted? A twenty-four-hour cable channel that shows nothing but Jane Fonda movies? I can't wait to catch *Barbarella* again.

Is she going to throw out the first javelin at the Goodwill Games? Show up on CNN doing leg lifts while spewing out left-wing commentaries.

Cool it with the sweat queen, Ted, and do something about your miserable excuse for a baseball team, or one night the Braves are going to give a game and absolutely nobody will show up.

Ted Turner and Jane Fonda. A match made in some foreign place where old bullpen catchers go to die.

15 ONE-SIZE-FITS-ALL GOVERNMENT

Freedom of expression is a wonderful
thing. That's why it shouldn't be against
the law to moon somebody.

I'll Moon You If You Burn Our Flag

I've been thinking about the implications of the recent Supreme Court ruling that says you can burn our flag and go unpunished.

The court ruled any law charging flag-burners with a crime is unconstitutional because the First Amendment protects freedom of speech and expression, no matter how distasteful and disgusting such actions might seem to others.

I can understand some of that. Make a law against burning the flag in protest, and that could lead to a law against burning down a post office in protest of long lines, surly workers, and the fact you just received a nice birthday card from your grandmother, who died in 1962.

Another part of me says, however, that no matter what the Supreme Court ruled, anybody who would burn our flag for any reason is a creep.

But we don't send people to jail just because they're creeps. If we did, our jails would be even more crowded than they already are.

They would be filled with such creepy people as filthy-mouthed rap singers, crooked politicians, and anybody who doesn't realize wrestling is fake—and the Rev. Al Sharpton.

I realize I am really waffling here, but it also seems to me like there ought to be something we could do to flag-burners.

Why do they have to burn our flag, our precious banner of freedom, sacrifice, and history, in the first place?

Couldn't they just burn a photograph of Dan Quayle instead?

I know what we could do to flag-burners instead of sending them to jail. We could send them all back to eleventh-grade American history class, where they would be assigned a term paper on Millard Fillmore.

And it would be due tomorrow. They might at least get a little respect for Old Glory through osmosis.

Regardless, I'd like to see them sweating over Fillmore's stance on the environment.

It also occurred to me—what sort of precedent is this ruling going to set? What other forms of speech and expression come under this ruling?

Can you, in fact, shout, "Fire!" in a crowded theater now?

And an even bigger question came to me: "Where does mooning come in here?"

Mooning is a form of expression, isn't it? You drop your drawers at your high school graduation ceremonies and you are expressing the thought "You can all stick it."

Let's say you're in the audience. Do you want the First Amendment tampered with regardless of how distasteful and disgusting it might be to have to look at some zit-faced kid's bare buttocks during "Pomp and Circumstance"?

If we are going to allow people to burn the flag and get away with it, we've got to let them shoot moons, too.

In fact, I'd rather be mooned than see somebody burning the flag. Furthermore, if I ever see somebody burning the flag, I'm going to moon him.

So, be forewarned. It will not be a pretty sight.

Nude Dance Parlors Have Nothing to Hide

Immediately upon hearing the Georgia Supreme Court had thrown out a law passed by the state legislature in 1988 making it illegal to serve alcohol in Atlanta's widely acclaimed nude-dancing parlors, I called my friend Rigsby, the man-about-town.

Had the law been upheld, the result likely would have been the closing of the clubs, once described as "internationally famous" by none other than the staid *Wall Street Journal.*

As for me, I do not frequent such places, preferring to remain home in the evenings trying to figure out the puzzles on *Wheel of Fortune,* then switching to the Arts and Entertainment channel to watch a good World War II documentary.

But not Rigsby. He is a regular at many of the clubs and has spent so much time looking at the nude dancers, he is currently at work on a book about the female anatomy titled *Mine Eyes Have Seen the Glory.* (His first title choice was *A Tale of Two . . . ,* but I talked him out of that one.)

Since the clubs received so much publicity after the law was passed, I figure business will pick up even more now, and I asked Rigsby what he might say to first-time visitors who don't know the ropes.

"I would be glad to help," said Rigsby. "First, don't try to see all the dancers at once."

"And why not?" I asked.

"Neck injury," he said. "A rookie walked into one club one night and there were thirty-eight girls dancing in the nude.

Rather than focusing on just one or two, he went for the entire enchilada and his head got stuck backward."

"I saw *The Exorcist*," I said. "This is a serious matter. What became of the man whose head was stuck backward?"

"He went to a chiropractor who turned his coat around," said Rigsby.

I continued my questions.

"The girls don't actually get completely naked, do they?"

"As jaybirds," answered Rigsby.

"I recall seeing strippers . . ."

"It's 'dancers,' " Rigsby interrupted. "The term 'strippers' is no longer operable. These ladies do not start with enough clothing on to be called strippers."

"Whatever," I said. "My question is, in the old days, such ladies tended to be slightly overweight, with holes in their stockings and a lot of bruises. What do today's dancers look like?"

"They'd make Vanna White look like a boy," said Rigsby. "You've simply got to get out more often. The war's been over nearly fifty years."

"But what about drugs and prostitution?" I asked. "The state legislature was quite concerned that such places would encourage the sale of drugs and prostitution."

"If it's drugs and prostitution you want, you have to go all the way out to the suburbs," said Rigsby.

"But isn't there a lot of, well, fondling going on?"

"Touch one of the dancers and a guy named Bruno will do the 'Beguine' on your head."

I had only one more question:

"You make the clubs seem quite appealing. Aren't they terribly crowded?"

"Only when the state legislature is in session," he said. "Then, you can't get a seat."

One-Size-Fits-All Government

During the recent budget crisis I kept hearing a lot about "nonessential government services."

"If Congress doesn't reach an agreement on the budget," the news anchors said, "then the nation faces a shutdown of nonessential governmental services."

So I started thinking. Just how many nonessential services does the government offer?

And, if these services are nonessential, it means we could get along without them, right?

And, if we could get along without them, then why do we have them in the first place, and wouldn't getting rid of them be a great place to start in reducing the federal deficit?

Couldn't even a looney tune like Newt Gingrich figure out such a simple premise?

So what governmental services are nonessential?

You've got your Washington tourist stops. They closed the Smithsonian during the budget crisis because there was no money to pay Smithsonian personnel.

Hasn't just about everybody seen all that stuff in the Smithsonian by now? We could box it up and store it someplace, and if anybody wanted to look at it again, they would be welcome to, as long as they were willing to go through the boxes and pull it out themselves.

The Washington Monument was closed, too. Why do we need to staff that? Want to see the Washington Monument? There it is. Stare as long as you please.

Air-traffic controllers we probably ought to keep, since I fly a lot. But do we really need all those people in post offices?

I don't care how many people you have working in a post office, you're still going to have to stand in line forever, anyway. So why not have half as many loafers? Heck, why not do away with the post office, altogether, and Fed Ex it?

We could give the national parks back to the bears. They were there first anyway. If anybody wanted to camp out, they could find a Motel 6 in some remote location and sleep on the floor.

Why doesn't Barbara Bush clean up behind that silly dog of hers herself so that the White House maid wouldn't have to come in but twice a week?

Want to look up something in the Library of Congress? They should have taught you the Dewey Decimal System in school. Look it up yourself and save the taxpayers some money.

Start talking nonessential and there's no end to it.

Do we really need a vice president with a big-bucks salary and a lot of perks? If anything happens to the president, just call in Alexander ("I'm in charge here") Haig until we can think of something. He would work free as long as we allow him to carry a swagger stick.

Couldn't we combine some Cabinet posts? Couldn't the secretary of state also handle interior? I ask you, was James Watt "essential"?

Why do we need Congress itself?

Let the governors get together once or twice a year and handle what would be a stripped-down, simplified, one-size-fits-all government.

You don't think this country couldn't get along without Newt Gingrich?

I think we've just solved a huge portion of the deficit problem here. Or, put it another way: Get a real job, Newt.

Tax 'Em Out on Their Assets

There's a big cry out there to tax the rich. In Congress they scream, "Tax the rich!" They don't mean it, of course, since they're all rich, but it sounds good and might get them reelected so they can come back to Washington and get even richer.

They say President Bush doesn't want to tax the rich. That's because he doesn't know anybody who isn't rich, and that wouldn't be a very nice way to treat your friends.

On the other hand, he could change his mind.

As for me, I certainly think the rich should do their part. But I don't think you can just say, "Tax the rich!"

Not every person who is rich got that way by the same route. The rich should be taxed at rates they deserve, and I have devised my own plan.

I don't think people who got rich because they were smart and thought of a great idea and then busted their tails to make the idea work should be harshly penalized for making a few million honest bucks.

I don't think people who rose from meager beginnings and worked eighteen hours a day, seven days a week for years until they finally made it should suffer unduly, either.

But there are groups of rich people I think we should stick it to. Send the IRS in with guns and just take what we think we need to help get us out of this financial mess we're in.

You asked for it, and here it is—The Rich People I'd Tax Out of Their Assets:

- The Lucky Sperm Club Rich: These are people who just happened to be born in the right place at the right time, the ones who caught the old Fallopian Tube of Fortune.

    Daddy did all the work, and now these little snits have the money. If they won't pay, the IRS should cut off the head of one of their polo ponies and put it in the bed with them. It's worked before.
- The Rock Star Rich: They make awful music and still get rich. Then they buy fourteen new cars and mansions with 612 rooms and then decorate each room with tacky furniture.

    I'd nail these people, too. Ten percent of their annual earnings for every sofa in their mansions that looks like it once was an animal that lived in or near a jungle.
- The Slime-Ball Rich: This would include dope and smut dealers, almost everybody currently involved in the film industry (Jessica Tandy being one of the exceptions), anybody who made a lot of money on the polyester hoax that was pulled on the country in the seventies, and the Rev. Al Sharpton. If he doesn't have a lot of money, just take what he has for being loud and obnoxious.
- The Couldn't-We-Have-Done-Without-Them Rich: Rich chiropractors.
- The Jock Rich: Mike Tyson, all boxing promoters, José Canseco, Deion Sanders, and anybody who holds out for 117 days and then signs for $20.5 million and later gives the credit to the Lord for helping him win the game. And George Steinbrenner.
- The Advertising Rich: Find whoever first thought of the phrase "new and improved" and take all his or her money. Also, put a big tax on car dealers who do their own TV commercials, and anybody who has ever done a commercial trying to push insurance off on old people—like Ed McMahon. He's got to be loaded in more ways than one.

- The Elected Rich: Find all the people who got rich after being elected to public office. First, tax them. Then, hang them.

Everybody who likes my plan can help by voting against an incumbent every chance they get.

Ku Klux
Klanner Unmasked

The Georgia State Supreme Court has rejected a Ku Klux Klan member's claim that he has a constitutional right to wear his KKK mask in public.

The court said wearing a mask can terrorize and intimidate. This from the chief justice:

"A nameless, faceless figure strikes terror in the human heart." Indeed.

Frankly, I've never trusted anybody wearing a mask. What's the face behind the mask hiding?

Take the Lone Ranger. Was he really Bernie Eisenstadt from New Rochelle, New York, running away from a morals charge involving two teenaged girls and a poodle dog named "Buffy"?

And what did "kemo sabe" really mean? "Lone, you rotten scuzbucket"?

The Georgia high court took the case after the Klansman, Shade Miller, Jr., (what a great name for a guy involved in a case like this—Shade) was arrested during a Klan demonstration for violating the state's antimask law, passed in 1951.

There is likely to be a subsequent appeal to the United States

Supreme Court, but I've got to believe the Georgia court's ruling will stand.

If these Klods are so dedicated to their long-lost causes, why do they want to wear masks in the first place?

What happened at the first Klan meeting ever?

Did one of the Klansmen suggest to the Grand Lizard, "This is pretty backward stuff. Maybe we ought to wear masks. If we don't, we might get kicked out of Rotary"?

While we're at it, I think we ought to do away with the rest of the Klan garb.

What are those silly robes all about? Judges, clergymen, and choir members ought to be the only people allowed to wear robes in public.

You see somebody wearing a robe in public and it can be pretty intimidating, too.

What's under that robe? Is this guy on his way to rob a bank with an AK-47 hidden under there?

Or maybe he's just stolen a pig or he's naked underneath and is out for a few flashes.

We ought to make the Klan take off those silly-looking pointed hats, too. Where do you go to buy one of those things anyway? The KKK mart?

Nobody has worn pointed hats since the castle wizards during the Dark Ages. They went out with burlap rags for serfs, who started wearing polyester rags.

Not only did they look better, but also they seriously cut down the itching factor.

Not only do I hope the Supreme Court upholds the Georgia ruling, I wish it would order that when the Klan demonstrates, it wear leisure suits with name tags that say, "Hello, my name is Spooky Gildenhammer, and I'm still living in the Dark Ages."

Said the Georgia chief justice:

". . . Remove the mask and the nightmarish form is reduced to its true dimensions. The face betrays not only identity, but also human frailty."

My way of saying that is, put the Klan in leisure suits with name tags and they won't be able to scare anybody ever again. We'll be too busy laughing at the Krapheads.

All of which reminds me of the time somebody walked up to my boyhood friend and idol, Weyman C. Wannamaker, Jr., a great American, and said, "Folks have been saying you're a member of the Ku Klux Klan."

Replied Weyman, "You misunderstood. What they've been saying is, I'm a booger under the sheets."

16 STUCK IN THE SAND IN THE MIDDLE EAST

Desert Storm, and one leftover line from whoever makes us such: What does an Iraqi boy do first when he becomes a man? Puts his diaper on his head.

A Trip Tease to the Middle East

Still got some vacation time left before summer's end and you want to go somewhere exotic and exciting?

Well, why not try the Middle East?

You don't want to risk going to San Francisco. When is the next Big One going to hit?

You don't want to go to New York since they outlawed your AK-47. Plus, there's the alligators in the sewers.

I know you're saying, "But isn't there a war or something going on in the Middle East?"

It's not really a *war*. Nobody's actually shooting at anybody yet.

Iraqi president and minister of tourism Saddam Hussein (pronounced "who sane"), was just kidding when he made that remark about plucking out our eyes.

Insiders say President Hussein is a real jokester who is always talking about plucking out an eye or two. It's his way of saying, "Come to Iraq, mon."

In fact, the best bargains for today's travelers are in Iraq. Oil revenues are down, and for a limited time, there are huge discounts being offered at Iraqi hotels.

At the Hotel Eye Plucker, American tourists may want to

choose the Great Satan Plan, which includes lodging, three meals, and a chance to go on Iraqi television and chant anti-Arab slogans such as, "You pluck out our eyes and we'll gouge out your gallbladders," for only $37.50 per day.

There are also some superbargain prices on airline tickets to the Middle East now, as long as you book them with Air Terror, the preferred airline of thrill-seekers from all over the world.

If Iraq isn't your cup of sand, there's Saudi Arabia, where Americans are always welcome, especially right now and especially if the Americans might be carrying a large rifle or driving a tank.

You think Daytona has a neat beach? The whole country of Saudi Arabia is a beach.

If you don't happen to have a tank, then you can still take a bus into the interior of Saudi Arabia and maybe catch one of those wondrous desert sandstorms.

The kids will enjoy the optical distortions if you are lucky and the temperature goes over 120 degrees.

But a tip for the happy traveler:

Take a few items like sunscreen and six gallons of water per day per family member.

If a war does break out while you're in Saudi Arabia, hide behind a big oil tank. Nobody's going to bomb that.

Or try visiting one of the sultanates in the region. One travel bureau has a slogan, "Oman! What a country!"

Or how about Turkey? Most Turkish prisons offer excellent bed-and-breakfast deals. You get your own queen-size slab, and gruel is served from 5:00 until 7:00 A.M.

All over the Persian Gulf area you are likely to run into interesting and intriguing native customs, like witnessing the beheading of a murderer or seeing a convicted thief get his hand chopped off.

"Wow!" the kids will say. "You never see any good stuff like this in Judge Wapner's court."

There's also Iran. See Ayatollah World where actresses and

actors re-create the taking of the American hostages in twice-daily performances and ride the famous Waterslide of Death.

The only place I wouldn't try is Kuwait. It's just not what it used to be after the looting.

So, go for it. Break a leg! Or, as they say in Iraq, "Pluck an eye!"

What Are We Brewing in Saudi Arabia?

It must be getting thirsty in Saudi Arabia by now. We've got all those American fighting troops over there, and they're not allowed to have any beer.

The Saudis don't believe in beer. I'm not certain such a country is worth defending, even against Saddam Hussein.

How can you stick all those soldiers out in the middle of the desert and not provide them a little beer occasionally?

The Saudis also will not allow anybody to send any nude photos to our kids. They probably can live with that. You can go without nude photos a lot longer than you can go without beer.

Don't get me wrong. Nude photos are okay, but they won't wash the sand off your tonsils.

Ever hear anybody say after a round of golf or a game of tennis or a twenty-mile march in 120-degree heat, "I'll have a nude photo, please"?

No, they want beer.

You may not realize this, but beer has played a big part in the military history of this country.

When Washington crossed the Delaware, he took a six-pack, which he drank along the way. That's how he drummed up the courage to stand up there in front of the boat.

When aides complained to President Lincoln that U. S. Grant was drinking too much during the Civil War, Lincoln asked, "What does he drink?"

The aides answered, "Miller Lite."

"Because it's less filling or has more taste?" asked Lincoln.

"He likes the can," they answered.

"Doesn't matter," said Lincoln. "Order each of my generals a case. Maybe they'll learn to fight like Grant."

The real reason Teddy Roosevelt and the Rough Riders charged up San Juan Hill was because somebody told them there was an iced-down keg of beer at the top.

I'm not certain how much our brave fighting women in Saudi Arabia miss beer, but you get a couple of hundred thousand guys together, for whatever reason, and they're going to want a few cold ones.

The lack of beer has got to be hurting morale. If I were George Bush, I'd level with the Saudis.

I'd tell them, "Read my lips. My boys have got to have some beer."

Can you imagine being twenty-two years old, being sent to a glorified sandbox and not knowing when you'll get home or even *if* you'll get home, and some guy dressed in something that looks like he stole off a bed in a Holiday Inn telling you that you can't have a lousy beer after you get off duty?

This is ridiculous. This is unfair. This is an issue that should have come up before and the president should deal with now.

I'm serious. Tell the Saudis to stick it.

If the government won't pick up the tab, I'm certain the American people will be willing to foot the bill for a beer lift to Saudi Arabia.

What are the Saudis going to do if we ignore their no-beer rule? Ask us to leave and have to depend on shaky allies to defend them against Saddam Hussein?

Of course not.

Tell 'em to kiss our Buds and go drink their oil.

Let's Go
Get 'Em

What this country has needed for a long time is to kick butt.

The last time we did it was in World War II. We showed 'em back then. With some help from our friends, we brought Hitler down and then we dropped a couple of big ones on Japan.

I still enjoy seeing the film of the Japanese officials signing their country's surrender.

Hey, guys, what did you expect? You sneaked in at Pearl Harbor and you bombed our navy and you killed our people and you thought you were going to get away with that?

No way. We didn't pussyfoot in those days. You started it, we finished it, and I always get angry when I read about commemorative protests against the United States's decision to dispatch the *Enola Gay* with its surprise. We were tough back then. Mess with us and you'll be immensely sorry.

But then came Korea. And then came Vietnam. Two dirty little wars that ended in scoreless ties.

We've seen our country scorned. We've seen our people taken hostage. We've seen our young soldiers die at the hands of terrorists with bombs.

Oh, we've issued a few sanctions here and there. We've warned our enemies that if they take one more step, we're going to intervene militarily, but we rarely do. Recall the phrase "paper tiger"? That's us. We've been all hat, no cattle.

But now's our chance. Iraq needs to go down in the worst sort of way. Iraq is a bully of a nation that engulfs its neighbors. It encourages terrorism. It uses poison gas. It is run by a devil.

In Europe they are calling Saddam Hussein "the new Hitler."

Hitler first bullied Austria and Czechoslovakia and nobody did anything. So he kept up his threats until the rest of the world finally figured out they were dealing with a bloodthirsty despot who eventually would try to take over the entire world if somebody didn't act to stop him.

Now, there is Saddam Hussein and Iraq. First, Kuwait. Who's next? Jordan, Saudi Arabia, and Israel?

Nobody could imagine Hitler going any further after he humiliated the British and the French in the Munich Agreement of 1938, but he did. He was a bud begging to be nipped, as is Hussein in Iraq.

Let's go get 'em. Get the Soviets to help as they did in World War II. Get the Israelis. Talk about a fighting machine. Israel, when it fears it is being threatened, wastes no time. It shoots first, asks questions later.

Let's go into Iraq. Let's send a message that says we're back, and we won't tolerate such aggression.

Over there, pal. That's where we need to be. Send in the marines. Put our top guns in their jets with orders to shoot to kill. Teach Iraq a lesson we taught the Germans and the Japanese.

They are just sitting over there asking for it. So let's answer back. Let's kick butt and take some names.

The world would be a safer place as a result. And whatever is left of Jimmy Carter's malaise would be swept away by our flag hanging high in Baghdad.

The Speech Police
on Patrol

Washington humorist Mark Russell was on one of those network morning news shows, and he was asked if he thought he could get away with humor based on the war with Iraq.

He said something like, "As long as I aim it at the enemy."

When he gave that answer, there was no war. The marshal (us) and the gunslinger (them) hadn't cleared leather yet. They were still standing in the empty street staring at one another.

But I thought the question was a good one.

You can't get away with very much anymore in a newspaper column, onstage, in a movie, or on radio and television without fear you'll say or write something the Speech Police won't like.

The Speech Police are on constant guard against remarks—humorous or otherwise—they consider to fall into those odious categories such as sexism, racism, xenophobia (the fear of foreigners), and homophobia (the fear of turning on Donahue and hearing guys complain because they can't get a marriage license and marry one another).

The Speech Police is made up of do-gooders, minority leaders, and the media.

They are the ones who want us to say "chairperson" instead of "chairman," and I'm still not sure if it's "black" or "Afro-American" now.

I once had a shortened version of "Japanese" that was popular in World War II thrown out of a column because "it would be offensive to the Japanese community."

I argued, "But I haven't forgiven them for sneaking up on us at Pearl Harbor."

I was told the fact I would use the term "sneaky" showed my xenophobia and even racist tendencies.

As far as homophobia goes, I've made it a policy never to refer to any sexuality that isn't hetero ever again. It's the only sort of sexuality I'm vaguely familiar with anyway.

But what happens now that there is a war with Iraq? What if thousands of American soldiers die trying to run Saddam Hussein out of Kuwait?

Isn't it okay to hate and fear Saddam Hussein now that he has brutally paraded our captured pilots?

You've noticed Jane Fonda hasn't said a word in behalf of Hussein and Iraq. If Hanoi Jane isn't backing them, then it must be okay for us to hate them and fear them and demean them.

Can I call Saddam Hussein an "arrogant, egotistical, savage 'towelhead,' " and sneak it past the Speech Police?

What if Hussein's soldiers attack Americans with chemical weapons and some of them die an awful, painful death in the desert?

Can I call them "cowardly camel jockeys" and get that past the Speech Police? There are precedents.

We had a name for both the Japanese and the Germans in World War II, and they were freely used in the public domain.

We laughed at Italy's soldiers and their cowardice. My father used a G-word in referring to the people he fought in Korea. The same term was a Vietnam favorite, too.

And can I make jokes about Saddam Hussein and his miserable country?

How about, "What do you get if you cross Saddam Hussein and a pig? Nothing. The pig would never agree to it."

And on top of that, does the Iraqi foreign minister, whose name sounds like a bowel disorder, wear one of those fake glasses, nose, and mustache gags, or is he just naturally that ugly?

I'll be waiting to hear from the Speech Police.

War on TV
Doesn't "Ad" Up

I've been watching a lot of television in an effort to keep up with the war. I've probably watched more television the first week of the war than I had watched all the previous years.

To be honest about it, however, I haven't learned a lot about the war by watching television.

Military censorship, of course, has a lot to do with that. And this war, so far, has been mostly air attacks at night, and if the Iraqis can't see the planes, how can I expect to see them eight thousand miles away on my television?

What I have learned, however, is if I have to watch a *Sports Illustrated* commercial giving away the Muhammad Ali videotape much longer, I'll be punch-drunk and loop-legged myself.

If you've watched television at all the last week, you've seen that SI commercial.

It's had more airtime than Bernie Shaw.

Here's the pitch:

It's an alleged bargain. You start a subscription to *Sports Illustrated* and you get a videotape of Muhammad Ali's big fights FREE!

The commercial was shot in Las Vegas, "Fight capital of the world."

So what else you have is all these people in the streets of Vegas talking about the tape.

These people are all incredibly excited about it. "Free! How can this be free?" one guy gushes.

And he's trying to win at the tables?

"It's not free, you ninny," I say to my television. "You've got to pay for your subscription, the videotape didn't cost *Sports Illustrated* very much in the first place, and Time-Life stands to make a lot of money here."

Where does *Sports Illustrated* find these people? Remember the sneaker-phone commercial?

It preceded the Ali spot. You subscribe to *Sports Illustrated* and you get a telephone shaped like a sneaker. FREE!

"It's a phone?" some dingbat asks. "This is great! Fantastic!"

Aren't these people a little too old to get that fired up over a telephone shaped like a shoe?

I saw a phone shaped like a beer can once. I didn't get fired up about it, however. In fact, I thought it was stupid.

Don't get me wrong, I like *Sports Illustrated*. I even worked for *Sports Illustrated* once.

The photography is wonderful. The writing and editing are superb. But just because I like to read about Joe Montana or digest a thoughtful piece about what's wrong with college football, it doesn't mean I'm some sort of juvenile who'd want a telephone shaped like what Michael Jordan wears on his feet to work.

Advertising can turn a consumer off. I don't buy anything that is supposed to be "new and improved."

Why didn't they get it right the first time?

I'd never buy a car from a car dealer who does his own commercials, go to a lawyer who has to go on television to get clients, and isn't one laxative about like all the others?

Now, I click the button on my remote the moment the Ali ad appears on my screen, which is about eighteen times a night. I've just about worn out my clicker trigger finger trying to escape it.

"Float like a butterfly, sting like a bee." Not a Patriot knocking out a Scud. Ali decking Sonny Liston again. Enough is enough.

I may drop my subscription to *Sports Illustrated* and use the money to buy an airline. Talk about a bargain.

Ways to Wipe Out Saddam and Gomorrah

There ought to be a way to take Saddam Hussein out.

Remember in *Godfather II* when Michael Corleone wanted to have that guy named Heime whacked?

One of his lieutenants says it's impossible. Too many FBI agents guarding him.

"Nothing," says Michael Corleone "is impossible."

Sure enough. They whacked Heime right there in the Miami airport. The guy who did the whacking got whacked himself, but Michael Corleone was right about the impossible bit.

You've got to figure if somebody took out Saddam, the war with Iraq would come to a quicker end and a lot of lives—Iraqis as well as America's allies and ours—would be saved.

Saddam Hussein is a bully. A torturer. A murderer. An egotistical maniac. Sort of a twentieth-century Attila the Hun with missiles, tanks, and bombs.

I certainly don't think God would think less of the person or persons who hit Saddam. I think God himself would say at a CNN briefing, "It's still 'Thou shalt not kill,' but sometimes you've got to be a little flexible."

(I would make up some quotes for Allah, but I can't type in Arabic.)

So, how to get Saddam. I thought of a few scenarios:

- Scenario #1: His own people get him. His generals, maybe. Or all the people of Iraq who are tired of war, tired of death, tired of eating sand. They revolt, track down Saddam, and cut off his head.

There hasn't been a good beheading that I know of in years and years.

• Scenario #2: The Israelis get him. The Israelis have been uncharacteristically patient while Saddam has hurled missiles at them.

But when the Israelis finally get enough, they strike swiftly and terribly.

I can see a Raid on Entebbe sort of thing where a group of crack Israeli commandos find Saddam and make him swallow a grenade.

• Scenario #3: We get him. We've got bombs smarter than the average Iraqi soldier.

So why can't we figure out where Saddam is and blow the place up with him in it? Or better yet, go in and get him and bring him back to this country and put him in the same cell with Jim Bakker.

• Scenario #4: Muhammad Ali gets him. Muhammad went to see Saddam and got some hostages out before the war. The two men embraced.

Muhammad could go back over armed with plastic explosives under his coat. When he and Saddam embrace again, Muhammad pulls a string inside his coat and no more Saddam.

No more Muhammad Ali, either. I need to work a little more on this one.

• Scenario #5: His wife gets him. Mrs. Saddam finally gets enough of her husband's bad humor, ill manners, and bullying tactics and poisons his soup.

He dies, she takes over the country and announces the immediate pullout from Kuwait and wants Baghdad to have a franchise in the new World Football League.

Nothing is impossible.

The Ultimate Gut Check

The television reporter was talking to a few good kid-marines in Saudi Arabia as The Deadline neared.

What an appropriate term I was thinking. Dead-line.

One young man had this to say: "I've never had a bullet fired at me, and have never fired at anyone else. I've been through training, but I've never been in the real thing.

"I just hope when it all starts I'll be able to do my job and be just as ready to die as the Iraqi soldier I'm fighting."

What the young man was saying was he hoped when the shooting started, he wouldn't be a coward.

How many times I've thought that myself. Combat must be the ultimate test of courage, the ultimate gut check.

Facing that test, would I scream and cry and run the other way? Or would I stand and fight?

A physical problem kept me out of Vietnam, and I'm too old for the Persian Gulf. I'm not complaining, but I'll never know the answer.

But still that question lingers. Bombs exploding around me. Bullets whizzing through the air.

Noise. Blood. Death. Hell. Could I have hacked it?

I know a man who is a few years older than I am. I consider him to be one of the strongest individuals I've ever met.

I'm seen him handle countless adversities with amazing courage.

He remains calm in the midst of madness. His is always the

voice of reason. If ever I had to follow someone into battle, I would want it to be him.

But he told me this once:

"I really wanted a career in the service. I went into the army out of college, a few years before Korea.

"But when my father died, I had to leave and go back home to take care of the family. A million times since, I've wondered if I'd stayed in and had been sent to Korea how I would have handled it.

"Until you've been in combat, you'll never know the limits of your courage. I might have just turned tail and run."

So I sit and watch that television and see and hear those kids. I think about my own father.

He was in World War II and then went back to Korea. He passed the test. In two wars. I have his Silver Star and his Purple Heart framed on my wall as proof.

But can courage be passed on genetically? I've gone into two heart surgeries without screaming and crying and kicking.

That's a big deal? Nobody was trying to kill me. They were trying to *save* my life.

All this "support for our boys" is a nice thing. Tie your yellow ribbons and wave your flags.

But also know and appreciate and pray that deep in hundreds of thousands of minds, souls, and hearts in that godforsaken desert that unsettling question is repeating itself over and over.

How will I handle it when they start shooting real bullets?

The strain must be overwhelming, the anxiety a mountain.

May God help them all. Wrestling with such a hideous unknown must be a hell all its own.

You Gotta Drawer the Line Somewhere

A report by Knight-Ridder newspapers said it's costing $750 million a day to operate Operation Desert Storm.

Of course, the U.S., which stands for Ultimate Sugar Daddy, is paying for most of it.

It is difficult for me to deal with a notion like $750 million a day. Even "$750 million a month" is bewildering.

I probably could handle "$750 million a decade," because that's what the average baseball player makes these days.

I was further confused by a graphic that accompanied the Knight-Ridder article.

It pictured an American male soldier in full combat gear and what each part of that gear cost. Here're some examples:

- Desert helmet: $103.
- Helmet cover: $2.50.
- Boots: $33.20.
- Socks: $1.65.
- M-16 rifle: $475.
- Two-quart canteen: $5.45.
- Canteen cover: $8.75.
- Belt: $6.60.
- Suspenders: $6.95.

The total estimated cost of outfitting a U.S. soldier came to $1,452.10.

There were a few things in the graphic I had to question.

One is, why does a canteen cover ($8.95) cost more than the canteen itself ($5.45)?

And if we issue a soldier a belt ($6.60), why does he also need suspenders ($6.95)?

The thing that concerned me most, however, was what we're paying for a soldier's drawers.

Out of the $1,412.10 being spent on the combat outfit, a measly $1.50 is spent on a soldier's underwear.

Have you priced men's drawers lately? Put a "Calvin Klein" or "Ralph Lauren" tag on them and they cost you twenty bucks or more.

Nondesigner drawers cost anywhere from ten to eighteen bucks.

And the ones we're giving our soldiers cost only a dollar-fifty?

There's nothing worse than a cheap pair of drawers. Wear them a couple of times and the elastic waistband stretches and suddenly you're wearing a most annoying and uncomfortable piece of clothing, commonly known as "droopy drawers."

It's tough just going to work in droopy drawers.

Ten times a day they fall down from the waist to just north of the knees. You have to go to the men's room, take off your pants, and pull up your drawers.

This causes the loss of valuable time in the workplace, not to mention considerable irritability.

Imagine how it would be to try and fight a war while wearing droopy drawers?

You can't just stop in the desert, pull down your desert trousers ($14.40), and pull up your droopy drawers.

I couldn't locate a military expert, retired or otherwise, to speak on this subject. They were all tied up with the networks.

But I think it is a damnable shame we don't think enough of our boys on the battlefront to give them a proper, functional pair of drawers.

It's just like our government to go hog-wild on canteen covers and suspenders, but basically ignore a much more important item, underwear.

I don't know what we can do here at home unless it's this: If you've got a man in the desert, send him some drawers.

Even if you can't afford Calvins or Ralphs, there are many more less-expensive fruits of the looms available, and they won't become droopy.

Operation Desert Drawers. It's time to act.

Notes from the Home Front:

- I was standing at the counter of a convenience store waiting to pay for my coffee. On the counter was a box of condoms.

  The picture on the front of the box was of a woman holding a baby. The baby had the face of Saddam Hussein.

  Underneath the picture it read: "Don't take a chance on bringing another Saddam Hussein into the world."
- My favorite name in the war: CNN's Wolf Blitzer. If only he were a linebacker.
- Has anybody else noticed how much General Swathmore looks like he was separated at birth from Jonathan Winters and Willard Scott?
- Read Lee Montville's piece on sports and war in *Sports Illustrated.* You won't be nearly as concerned about the fact that Isiah Thomas is out for the Detroit Pistons.
- I want to see a headline that reads: U.S. BOMBS IRAQ AROUND THE CLOCK.
- Media complaints about military secrecy are sort of stupid. There are lives at stake.

  Did Eisenhower call a press conference before D-Day and advise the press corps, "Our plans are to hit the beach at

Normandy but don't tell Hitler. He thinks we're landing at Calais"?

Catch your Pulitzer covering another story.

- I heard two older guys talking. One said to the other, "They ought to bring those young boys back from over there so they can produce some babies. They ought to send dried-up folks like us over there. We're going to die soon anyway."

The other guy listened and then replied, "You're crazy."

- Why is it cheaper for Iraq to train its pilots than it is for us to train ours? They don't have to teach theirs to land.

- First verse of a song I'm writing about the war for Hank Williams, Jr.:

"Saddam Husseiiiin/You're so damned insaaaane/You spilt our blood and you spilt the oil/and this here ol' boy is about to boil. . . ."

- A fighter pilot from the Vietnam era was telling me "pilot fatigue in a war comes from hearing too much and thinking too much about statistics and laws of average.

" 'What's my chances of coming back today?' That's what fatigues you, not the actual hours you're in your airplane."

- Is there any chance Dan Quayle's National Guard unit could be called up?

- Worst war song so far: The one that begins, "Bomb, bomb, bomb, bomb, bomb Iraq," sung to the tune of "Bah-bah-bah-bah bah berAnn . . ."

- I have a friend who made plans last summer to go to Europe for the first time later this month. "There were twenty-eight of us who signed up," she explained. "But because of the war there's just six of us left. Think we should go?"

I wouldn't. There will be lots of times later to see museums and cathedrals and get left by the last train to Milan.

- Read President Bush's lips: "This is no Vietnam."

It certainly isn't. Jane Fonda hasn't gone to Baghdad yet.

"Let's Get the Shell Outta Here!"

Two Iraqi soldiers, Hassan and Abdul (Iraqi for Frank and Arnold), were hunkered down in their bunker in Kuwait.

"We are certainly showing the infidels a thing or two, are we not, Abdul?" asks Hassan.

"The Great Satan soon will be brought to his knees, and we will pluck out his eyes and leave him to rot in the sun," replies Abdul.

An artillery shell from advancing coalition forces explodes a few yards from the bunker. Abdul recoils.

"Do not fear, my brave and devoted comrade," Hassan tells him. "Allah will not let harm come to us, for we are the Messengers of God, sent forth to bring death and disgrace to the criminal transgressors."

"You're absolutely sure about that, fellow crusader?" asks Abdul.

"On a scale of one to ten, about seven."

Another shell explodes.

"Better make that six, dear brother in the fight to send the evil intruders back home in sad coffins," Hassan corrects himself.

"Tell me the part about plucking out the eyes of the Great Satan," says Abdul. The nervousness in his voice gives him away.

"Do not tell me you are wavering on our mission to disembowel this hateful Enemy of God and all who love and praise him?" asks Hassan.

"Perhaps," answers Abdul, "if I had just had something to eat lately, my comrade standing shoulder to shoulder with me to liberate the sands of vermin that now moves swiftly across it, my morale would be higher."

Hassan is shocked.

"How can you think of the emptiness of your stomach," he asks, "as we prepare for the mother of all battles?"

"I am sorry, my heroic friend," Abdul apologizes, "but perhaps if I just had a goat sandwich or a handful of Frito . . ."

A third artillery shell explodes, even closer to the bunker of the two Iraqi soldiers. In the distance they can hear the rumble of approaching allied tanks, growing closer and closer.

"To be perfectly honest about it, my companion in faith," Abdul begins, "I've never had much interest in plucking out eyes."

"Are you certain we shouldn't think this thing over? The Great Satan might even have chicken noodle soup."

"Are you suggesting, my gallant and fearless warrior, that we surrender to the atheistic forces?" asks Hassan.

"Just a thought," is Abdul's answer. "I could eat the tonsils of a camel, and my shorts are filled with sand."

"But what would our Leader and Right Hand of God, Saddam Hussein, think of such cowardice?"

"That power-hungry idiot is the one who got us here in the first place," says Abdul. "I'm out of this jihad," he adds, tossing his rifle out of the bunker.

"Wait for me, Wise and Thoughtful One," says Hassan, "I will ask for Cheeseburger."

Let's Hear It for the Red, White, and Blue

Announcing the war in the Gulf had been won, President Bush, our esteemed and victorious commander in chief, said, ". . . It is not a time to gloat."

That's like telling Georgia Tech football fans, whose team won a national championship last season after a lot of years of being kicked around, they couldn't raise a glass and a finger and proclaim, "We're number 1."

Mr. President, Korea was a flop. Vietnam was worse. Iran took our citizens hostage and we couldn't do anything about it.

And for how many years now have we turned on our television sets to see Arab masses in the streets chanting anti-American slogans, burning our flag, and daring us to take one step in their direction?

Mr. President, with all due respect, I think there ought to be a national day of gloating.

Let the kids out of school. Close down workplaces. Cancel the National Hockey League schedule. Let's have parades and victory celebrations and get down to some real old-fashioned gloating.

We've got a lot to gloat about.

Saddam Hussein, my foot. (I can't say you-know-what in a family newspaper.)

He's a brilliant military commander? He's started two wars in the last ten years and lost them both.

That blustering, bullheaded, bloodthirsty booger of the burning sands.

He amassed the fourth-largest army in the world, and it took us one hundred hours on the ground to chop it to pieces.

I like what General Norman Schwarzkopf said of President Meathead.

"As far as Saddam Hussein being a great military strategist, he is neither a strategist nor is he schooled in operational arts, nor is he a general, nor is he a soldier. . . ."

Sounds like somebody assessing any number of Atlanta Falcons head coaches.

And the courageous Iraqi soldiers.

What a bunch of wimps. A television reporter was describing a dead and very flat Iraqi soldier smeared on a street in Kuwait City. "He appeared to have been run over by one of his own tanks in a hurry to get out of the city."

In that same report, somebody talked about Iraqi soldiers going into homes in Kuwait City looking for sheets or anything white with which to make flags of surrender.

Some Iraqi troops even surrendered to the press. That's like Hulk Hogan saying "Uncle" in a wrestling match with Regis Philbin.

And there were those grimy, beaten Iraqi prisoners raising their fists in the sky chanting, "George Bush! George Bush!"

If only the ayatollah lived long enough to have witnessed that.

We're back. We're strong, We're united. And we have stopped taking it and we've finally dished it out.

Go ahead and gloat all you want, is all I say. Gloat, cheer, and give thanks it's over "over there" and we, by God, whipped their Iraqi *Al-bagoongahs*, the Iraqi word for you-know-what.

Sorry, Mr. President. But it's party time.

Gulf War Notes

Closing the notebook of the War in the Gulf; a farewell to arms.

- Schwarzkopf for President. We haven't had a military person in the White House since Ike. How could anybody not vote for the man who won the War in the Gulf, Stormin' Norman?

  Only one way, if he ran as a Democrat.
- Beer: American troops had to do without for months as they served in Saudi Abstentia. Here's a great public-service idea:

  Why don't the big brewers give each returning soldier all the brew he or she can drink for a year? Call your local distributors with this patriotic suggestion.
- Misfire: The term from the war with the best chance of remaining a part of our language: "Scud."
- Suggested Next Assignment for Peter Arnett: Stationed inside the IRS as it decides who to audit.
- Suggested Punishment for Saddam Hussein in Hell: Bury his head in the camel dung pit for the first ten thousand years; then put him in the Rat, Snake, Spider, and Scorpion Room next to the ayatollah.
- Sweet Surrender: After hearing Iraqi soldiers had surrendered to an Italian news photographer, a guy said, "That's the first time in history the Italians have taken a prisoner of war."
- Suggested Next Assignment for Wolf Blitzer: Anything that

gets him away from reporting from in front of the same map for two months.

- Dan Quayle's Top Three Contributions to the War Effort: (1) He learned to dress himself every morning during the crisis, allowing Marlin Fitzwater more time to work on press briefings. (2) He stuck to the script prepared for him in speeches and didn't say one single incredibly stupid thing. (3) He stayed up to watch *Nightline* twice.
- Good Point: A mother wrote a newspaper suggesting another condition Iraq should be made to accept is changing the spelling of its country.

  "I've tried to teach my children a 'q' is always followed by a 'u,' " she wrote. "They watch war reports on television and tell me I'm wrong."
- That's What I Would Have Done: Reports said Iraqi soldiers broke into a Kuwait City communications center and hauled out a load of computers they thought were televisions. When they discovered they weren't, they smashed the screens.
- Best Clean Joke of the War: Quickest way to break up an Iraqi bingo game? Call B-52.
- Best Dirty Joke of the War: Has to do with an Iraqi with a pig under one arm and a sheep under the other. Use your imagination.
- Best President in Office During a War Since FDR: Big George.
- Best Headline I saw During the War: UNLEASHED, from the *Sunday Atlanta Journal and Constitution*, announcing the start of the ground campaign.
- Best Word to Appear in Any War Headline: PEACE.

LEWIS GRIZZARD had been described as "one of the foremost humorists in the country," "a Faulkner for plain folks," and "this generation's Mark Twain" by the national press. Lewis Grizzard is a masterful storyteller, standup comedian, syndicated columnist, and best-selling author.

Grizzard was born in Fort Benning, Georgia, and spent most of his youth in nearby Moreland. He says he was raised poor, proud, and patriotic. He is a graduate of the University of Georgia.

His books tend to "stir folks up" with a combination of outrageous humor and bittersweet stories of yesteryear. In this, his latest effort, the King of Humor and Wit creates scenes that will make you laugh and cry at the same time.

Books may be borrowed for ⚫weeks
Renewals will not be made
OVERDUE books will be charged for
at the rate of ⚫per day
The library is not responsible
for reminding you. The DATE
CARD in this pocket is your
reminder. Do not remove it

Union County Public Library
Monroe, North Carolina 28112